The Hipster Handbook

by **Robert Lanham**

Art by **Bret Nicely**

and **Jeff Bechtel**

Anchor Books

A Division of Random House, Inc.

New York

For Amy, my one true love.

FIRST ANCHOR BOOKS EDITION, FEBRUARY 2003

Copyright © 2002 by Robert Lanham
Illustrations copyright © 2002 by Bret Nicely and Jeff Bechtel

Additional editing done by Glenn Coan-Stevens

Library of Congress Cataloging-in-Publication Data
Lanham, Robert.
The hipster handbook / text by Robert Lanham ; illustrations by
Bret Nicely and Jeff Bechtel.—1st Anchor Books ed.
p.   cm.
ISBN 1-4000-3201-6
1. American wit and humor. I. Nicely, Bret. II. Bechtel, Jeff.
III. Title.
PN6165 .L36 2003
818'.602—dc21   2002028045

Book design by Mia Risberg

www.anchorbooks.com

Printed in the United States of America

Hipsters think straying from publishing conventions is cutting-edge
and postmodern so, to stay true to form, we have inserted some
content here:

Content

(You'll notice that inserting the word "content" challenges the notion of
what content is traditionally considered to be. This is also very artistic,
and therefore hip. We wanted to discuss in detail the font that we would
be using as well, but are running out of room. Sorry.)

10   9   8   7   6   5   4   3   2   1

Contents

Everything That Once
Was Cool Is Now Deck

You've seen them all over town with their mop-top haircuts, swinging retro pocketbooks, talking on cell phones, smoking European cigarettes, shading their eyes behind bug-eyed lenses, and strutting in platform shoes with a biography of Che sticking out of their bags. They come in all colors, shapes, sizes, and nationalities. Beck is one. Jack Kerouac was one. Meg from the White Stripes is one. And the girl at work in the Jackie-O dress is one too. You may even be one yourself. From New York to New Zealand, Hipsters are everywhere. Welcome to *The Hipster Handbook*, the first guide to what it means to be a Hipster.

Since Hipsters are a vital part of the international social fabric, this book is for everyone. If you are a Hipster yourself, carry it in your back pocket or in your purse. Excuse yourself to the bathroom during that important party and brush up on the correct lingo by consulting our glossary. Even Hipsters need a refresher course from time to time, and you wouldn't want to be throwing out dated slang like "grody" or "wicked" when mixing with other Hipsters in the know.

If you are not a Hipster, but want to learn more about this ubiquitous genus, this book is for you too. We will teach you how to spot Hipsters, how to interact with them, and how to better understand their unique culture. If you are a parent with Hipster children, this book will help you understand and maybe even talk to your children. You'll also become just a little more deck in the process. If you are a scientist, we hope you'll use our anthropological studies as a starting point to document the phenomenon of this emerging human archetype. Our research garnered us a nomination for the Margaret Mead Award in 2001.

And finally, this book is for those among you who want to become Hipsters yourselves. Anyone can become one with the proper education. Study this book and complete the questionnaire at the end and you will be on your way.

But perhaps we are being too kind in saying this book is for everyone. Some people are clearly hopeless. If you are a neo-Nazi and accessorize with an automatic weapon, this book is not for you. If you have appeared in the *Girls Gone Wild* video series, this book is not for you. If you go to tanning salons, this book is not for you. If you listen to Slipknot and have ever been to the Warped Tour, this book is not for you. And perhaps most important, if you are wearing a sweatshirt that has a Disney character on it, this book is not for you.

For everyone else, we present the long-overdue documentation of what it means to be deck—or, depending on your age, groovy, nifty, fresh, chic, savvy, fly, bodacious, jazzy, cool, righteous, hip, and hep. This is the motherfucking HIPSTER HANDBOOK.

11 Clues You Are a Hipster

1. You graduated from a liberal arts school whose football team hasn't won a game since the Reagan administration.
2. You frequently use the term "postmodern" (or its commonly used variation "PoMo") as an adjective, noun, and verb.

3. You carry a shoulder-strap messenger bag and have at one time or another worn a pair of horn-rimmed or Elvis Costello–style glasses.

4. You have refined taste and consider yourself exceptionally cultured, but have one pop vice (*ElimiDATE,* Quiet Riot, and *Entertainment Weekly* are popular ones) that helps to define you as well-rounded.

5. You have kissed someone of the same gender and often bring this up in casual conversation.

6. You spend much of your leisure time in bars and restaurants with monosyllabic names like Plant, Bound, and Shine.

7. You bought your dishes and a checkered tablecloth at a thrift shop to be kitschy, and often throw vegetarian dinner parties.

8. You have one Republican friend whom you always describe as being your "one Republican friend."

9. You enjoy complaining about gentrification even though you are responsible for it yourself.

10. Your hair looks best unwashed and you position your head on your pillow at night in a way that will really maximize your cowlicks.

11. You own records put out by Matador, DFA, Definitive Jux, Dischord, Warp, Thrill Jockey, Smells Like Records, and Drag City.

11 Clues You Are Not a Hipster

1. You teach Sunday School.
2. You use hair spray and wear pleated pants or pastel dress suits.
3. You are a big fan of the suburbs and vinyl siding.
4. You have a special "spill shirt" that you wear when you eat dinner at night.
5. You like to watch college football.
6. You read novels with raised lettering on their covers.
7. You eat at Popeye's on a regular basis.

Non-Hipsters

8. You like to listen to the Dave Matthews Band while driving in your SUV.
9. You wear holiday-themed sweaters with Santa Clauses, jack-o'-lanterns, and snowflake patterns knitted onto them.
10. You work in an office building that has a man-made pond and a fountain in its front lot.
11. You consider Jim Breuer to be a comic genius.

Who Says "Tubular" Anymore?

Like most social groups, Hipsters have their own way of communicating. They converse using special terms and lingo to show they are in the know. Being up on the latest slang is essential to being a Hipster. Though it may be humorous to tell someone that his or her Pumas are "tubular," utilizing a dated term such as this can be a serious faux pas if not used ironically. Retro terms such as "grody," "bofu," "trippendicular," and "wicked" all work well when with a tongue in cheek, but such words should be used sparingly.

Before you read any further, we recommend you take a quick peek at our glossary of terms, since many will be used throughout the book. With a little practice, we will help you turn an awkward sentence like "I'm gonna look bitchin' in my groovy jacket" into the much hipper "I'll polish in my deck flogger."

The Glossary:

bennie—hat. *Sentence:* "Have you seen Micah's new bennie? She looks deck as ef." "It's cold out today; I'd better grab my bennie."

berries—dollars (see also **kale**). *Sentence:* "Can I borrow a couple berries? I want to go to Diesel and pick up a new outfit."

Bipster—blue-collar Hipsters who shun art-school pretension and have little patience with leisure-class Hipsters (see page 112).

bleeker—tourist. *Sentence:* "Every time I'm in the city, some bleeker asks me for directions."

boggle—vomit. Origin: An exceptionally hip tassel in Atlanta once shook a Boggle cup to drown out the sound of her friend vomiting in the bathroom, which was making her feel ill as well. The term caught on.

bronson—beer. *Sentence:* "I drank a sixer of bronsons last night while watching the game." Origin: Watching Charles Bronson movies while drinking beer is deck. The term spawned from this ritual.

bust a moby—to dance. *Sentence:* "Let's go to the Tunnel and bust a moby." "Did you see her moves at the party last night? She really knows how to bust a moby."

Carpet—a lesbian Hipster (see page 57).

chipper—a woman who's easy. *Sentence:* "She's a real chipper and will sleep with anyone after one bronson."

chowder—alcoholic beverage, usually a mixed drink. *Sentence:* "The Pourhouse has half-price chowder until seven P.M. Let's get shellacked!"

Clubber—younger Hipsters from the Gen-Y set who love to dance, listen to electronic music, and promote parties (see page 26).

CK-1—a bisexual Hipster (see page 59).

clothesline—the gossip that is on the scene. *Sentence:* "Yo, I heard on the clothesline that she is sleeping with Billy. She is such a chipper."

cronkite—boy. *Sentence:* "Have you seen Anne's new cronkite? She met him at the café and he is such a frado."

deck—a key word for most Hipsters, similar in meaning to the antiquated "fresh." To be deck is to be up on the latest trends, cutting edge, and/or hip. *Sentence:* "That tassel we met at the gallery opening sure looked deck in her cowboy boots." "Have you checked out the new Jonathan Lethem book? It's deck."

fin—the opposite of deck, similar to outdated terms like "wack" and "lame." Something that is fin is bad or undesirable. *Sentence:* "How can you like that Vin Diesel movie? Every film he's ever starred in has been fin." "My date with Larry

A Chipper Giving a Cronkite the Frigidaire

6

was so fin. He took me to Applebee's and ordered cheese fries as an appetizer."

flavorless—heterosexual. *Sentence:* "He kinks his hair and wears tight pants, but he's definitely flavorless. He's been going out with the same tassel for nine months."

flogger—coat. *Sentence:* "I bought this wool flogger at the Salvation Army. It was only five berries!"

flubber—breast implants. *Sentence:* "There's no way they are real; those shits are flubber!" Origin: This term originated from the Disney movie *The Absent-Minded Professor,* in which eccentric chemist Fred MacMurray inadvertently creates a bouncing synthetic compound known as flubber (flying rubber).

frado—an ugly guy who thinks he's good-looking. *Sentence:* "Bill thinks all the girls love him, but they all know he's a frado."

A Frado

the frigidaire—the cold shoulder. *Sentence:* "I don't know what her problem is, but she gives me the frigidaire every time I see her."

get puffy—to bust a cap. *Sentence:* Actually, this phrase is never used. Hipsters are art-school kids.

gluten (pronounced **gloo-tin**)—to eat. *Sentence:* "I'm starving; let's gluten."

greaser—an individual who comes from somewhere with a small Hipster demographic (usually Jersey or Miami). *Sentence:* "Frank has a mullet and acts like a greaser when he's shellacked."

heat—pull or influence. *Sentence:* "Leesy has heat. She always gets us on the guest list."

hilfiger—having no fashion sense. *Sentence:* "You'd think he was broke, he dresses so hilfiger." Origin: Etymologists have come to the conclusion that this term originated from the Hipster consensus that Tommy Hilfiger is lame. Scientists, anthropologists, and fashion experts tend to concur that wearing Tommy Hilfiger is dorky.

Hipster—One who possesses tastes, social attitudes, and opinions deemed cool by the cool. (Note: it is no longer recommended that one use the term "cool"; a Hipster would instead say "deck.") The Hipster walks among the masses in daily life but is not a part of them and shuns or reduces to kitsch anything held dear by the mainstream. A Hipster ideally possesses no more than 2 percent body fat.

hypo—a cokehead. *Sentence:* "His Steven Seagal ponytail makes him look like a hypo, and I think I saw him wiping his nose."

ishtar—bad. *Sentence:* "Yo, that shit was ishtar."

jerry—a stoner, hippie. *Sentence:* "My pits smell totally ishtar. I feel like a jerry."

jug—a forty-ounce bottle of domestic beer. *Sentence:* "Tassels respect me. I can drink a whole jug and still bust a mean moby."

juicer—A ladies' man. An individual who has undeniable sex appeal. *Sentence:* "I wish he would ask me out; he's such a juicer."

kale—money (see also **berries**). *Sentence:* "Yo, Kim, can you slide me some kale? I'm still waiting for my mom to send rent."

kidsman—one who rounds up children to educate them in thievery. (Oops—this is Victorian slang, not Hipster slang.)

lilith—associated with clichés of lesbian culture. *Sentence:* "That bar has Tori Amos on the jukebox. How lilith can you get?!" Origin: The Lilith Tour sucked.

liquid (sometimes **liquefy**)—having performed a sexual act with another. *Sentence:* "I saw the way you looked at Marty. Are you two liquid?" "She's got such a tight bod. I'd love to liquefy that ass."

Loner—introverted Hipsters who have little time for social engagements due to a borderline obsessive relationship with their hobbies and/or work (see page 32).

Maxwell—a gay Hipster (see page 56).

midtown—uncultured or unhip. *Sentence:* "He's never heard of Spike Jonze. He's so midtown."

nancy—ass. *Sentence:* "Amy has a good head on her shoulders." "Maybe so, Mike, but have you seen her nancy?"

Neo-Crunch—post-Garcia hippies promoting idealism for a new century (see page 79).

piece—cell phone. *Sentence:* "I must have been on the subway; my piece didn't ring."

polish—impress. *Sentence:* "I'm gonna polish with my new modern mohawk do." "I was nervous for the interview, but my résumé polished."

Polit—extremely literary Hipsters who have philosophical approaches to politics and existence, but are romantic in matters of love. The term "Polit" (pronounced **pah**-lit) is an amalgamation of the words "political" and "literary" (see page 99).

raphaels—glasses. *Sentence:* "Do these raphaels go with my flogger? I don't know if I like the new frames or not."

riding greyhound—sour luck, to be put in a bad position. *Sentence:* "Ever since Todd got laid off, he has been broke." "Yeah, he's riding greyhound."

Schmooze—a networking Hipster obsessed with his/her career (see page 42).

semi—a partial erection. *Sentence:* "The movie at the Film Forum was steamy. Thank God I had popcorn to cover my semi."

shellacked—drunk. *Sentence:* "I was so shellacked last night that I lost count of how many chowders I drank!"

tassel—girl. *Sentence:* "Jim is definitely a frado, but somehow he gets a new tassel every night."

Teeter—young-at-heart Hipsters who are most commonly associated with skateboards, graffiti, and tagging (see page 90).

A Shellacked Cronkite

uni—university. *Sentence:* "Jane is nice but I just can't be friends with someone who went to a public uni."

UTF (Unemployed Trust-Funder)—Hipsters who have the benefit of a wealthy family and are thus unencumbered by the distraction of a "straight" job (see page 14).

vejjo—vegetarian. *Sentence:* "I would never go to Mike's Steakhouse! Nothing there is vejjo."

wally—an attractive male Hipster. *Sentence:* "Have you seen Jennifer's brother? He's a definite wally." Origin: some say this is an acronym for Women Always Look Longingly at You. Others claim that "wally" is a reference to the character on *Leave It to Beaver.*

WASH (Waitstaff and Service Hipster)—Hipsters who work as bartenders, waiters/waitresses, in coffee shops, and sometimes at record and video stores (see page 66).

Phrases and Terms
Avoided by Hipsters

1. Having lunch with the big boys
2. Heavens to murgatroyd
3. Beam me up, Scotty
4. Ducks in a row
5. Whistling "Dixie"
6. Postgay
7. Put my kahunas on the line
8. Da bomb
9. Poon
10. Anywho
11. Pipe down
12. Think outside the box
13. Gotta be jelly 'cause jam don't shake like that
14. Cool beans
15. H-E-double-hockey-sticks
16. Cowabunga
17. Ba da bing
18. Mind your P's and Q's
19. Jumping Jehoshaphat
20. Shiver me timbers
21. Bustin' your chops
22. Hip hip hurray
23. Playa Hata
24. Crikey
25. Panties

Core Elements of Hipsterdom

Given their varying backgrounds and lifestyles, it is not surprising that Hipsters come in many different forms. There are, however, several core elements essential to being a Hipster.

- Hipsters are always very conscious of what they are wearing and distinguish themselves by dressing creatively. Whether they set the standard for what will be on the cover of *GQ* and *Vogue*, sport a retro fashion look that combines kitsch with good taste, or dress casually in crunchy hippie gear, all Hipsters choose a personal style for themselves that helps them to stand apart from the masses. Why so many Hipsters tend to look like each other is a subject for another discussion.
- Hipsters possess an innate contempt for franchises, strip malls, and the corporate world in general. Their sharpest disdain, though, is reserved for the SUV, which they think is an acronym for "smog unleashing vehicle."
- Hipsters take their music collections very, very seriously. Many shape their wardrobe, and often even their personalities, to match the music they like. Just look at metal heads, mods, electroclashers, and punks. With few exceptions, Hipsters listen solely to bands produced by independent labels and steer clear of major labels such as Island and Capitol. It's easy to spot Hipsters in the personals; instead of describing their hair and eye color, they say "I like Cave-In and the Clash."
- Hipsters believe that irony has more resonance than reason.

- Hipsters are artists who always lean to the left politically. Republican Hipsters are about as silly as Jews for Jesus. Hipsters tend to be champions of the First Amendment, the quintessential Lefty political cause. They are also into social causes and the environment, issues that are traditionally not embraced by the Right. More conservative Hipsters are into the Libertarian party. More extreme Hipsters are Socialists. And though radical and unrealistic worldviews such as anarchism are generally considered to be pretty fin, you will nonetheless be hard-pressed to find a Hipster who supports George Bush. Most think Ted Nugent is pretty cool, though, despite his NRA connections.
- Hipsters never admit to being Hipsters. They are too cool to broach the subject.
- Hipsters are always more culturally aware than most. They enjoy Tibetan, Vietnamese, Moroccan, and American food with equal zest. They know the difference between pinot noir and cabernet sauvignon. They know that *Titanic* is a lame movie and that *Buffalo 66* is deck. They know that John Grisham is shit and they dig Martin Amis. They know that *Wallpaper* is a better read than *Maxim*, though *Italian Maxim* can be deck.
- Hipsters understand that cultural trends become fin the moment they hit the mainstream. Many Hipsters still like Radiohead, but they know better than to say so. Hipsters also enjoy declaring random things, like vodka martinis or exercise, passé.
- Hipsters think lists like this one suck ass.

Underneath their apparent individualism, Hipsters conform just like everyone else. They can be classified into ten core personality types: the UTF (page 14); the WASH (page 66); the Loner (page 32); the Schmooze (page 42); Maxwells, CK-1's, and Carpets (page 56); the Teeter (page 90); the Neo-Crunch (page 79); the Clubber (page 26); the Polit (page 99); and the Bipster (page 112).

The UTF (Unemployed Trust-Funder)

Definition—Hipsters who have the benefit of a wealthy family and are thus unencumbered by the distraction of a "straight" job.

Question: Are you a Hipster?
Answer: I'm totally bohemian. Instead of spending my berries on Helmut Lang, I bought this authentic Rick Springfield concert shirt at a yard sale. Check it out; it's deck as ef.

ATTIRE/PRESENTATION

Dressing in secondhand clothes from thrift shops allows the UTF to travel like a chameleon from one social class to the next without anyone batting an eye. They rarely buy fancy designer duds, leather jackets, or shoes from Prada. UTFs experience being bohemian by dressing the part. The UTF male knows that a greasy 'do and a secondhand work shirt go a long way. The UTF female knows the value of a musky armpit and will on occasion forgo a shower or two. Many accessorize with a vanity item such as a silver cigarette case, which they usually say they found on the street.

BACKGROUND AND UPBRINGING

UTFs usually grow up in cities or in suburbs in close proximity to large urban centers. They have close relationships with their parents and adopt their sensibly liberal views as their own. Many secretly resent their parents, though, for taking them out of public school when they were young. They often call their fathers "my old man" to show a distanced fondness. UTFs always avoid calling their fathers "daddy," a cliché that would hint at their status as part of a wealthier class. UTF siblings are often best friends, creating conjecture and suspicion about the true nature of their relationship.

PHILOSOPHY AND BELIEFS
Not shampooing speaks louder than words.
Free speech for the Left!
NPR is a pillar of objective journalism.

DISPOSITION
Cheerful. In public, UTFs are great communicators, often relating extravagant travel stories from exotic places such as Bali and Thailand and flavoring any conversation with humor. Behind closed doors, UTFs can become smug, criticizing those who don't have cell phones or asking the pizza delivery man to take out the garbage.

AVERSION
State universities.

FORM OF TRAVEL
Mopeds, especially used Vespas to avoid being ostentatious.

THE HOME
UTFs do not travel too far from home when deciding where to put a down payment on their first mortgage, usually in their mid-twenties. Most decorate minimally, since much of their time is spent abroad or working in their studios on conceptual art pieces. Most are very messy and grew up with housekeepers. On the rare occasion they do their own laundry, they have to read the instructions on the machine.

EDUCATION AND CAREER
UTFs basically attend any school they want, since their parents have disposable incomes and influence. Members of admissions boards who reject the applications of UTFs have been known to "disappear." Most UTFs choose a program that will provide them a semester or two overseas. Parents of some UTFs dish out a dose of tough love by

cutting back on the amount of money they give their children after graduation, merely sending enough to cover rent. They rarely work, and understand that being deck is a full-time job.

POPULAR WAYS UTFS
DISGUISE THEIR UPPER-CLASS STATUS

- Driving a hearse or a mail car bought at an auction
- Taking a summer job on a lobster boat
- Drinking forty-ouncers and Tab soda
- Stocking the fridge with generic brands
- Borrowing money
- Grabbing the mail before anyone notices their "letters" from home
- Saying "I'm a freelancer"
- Clipping coupons for the market
- Becoming a full-time student
- Biting their nails
- Reading the classifieds
- Whittling

DATING A UTF

Common Turn-ons—playing badminton or croquet, chipped front teeth, a subscription to *Harper's* magazine, decorative Vespa goggles, people from New England

Major Turnoff—muscles

UTFs love to talk about art. Speak to them knowingly about painting, sculpture, and photography and you will never fail to impress. Their art-school backgrounds lead them into lengthy discussions about postmodernism and postfeminism; actually, add "post" to just about anything and you'll see them squirm in their chairs with excitement. UTFs are aroused by understated behavior and feel uncomfortable when around rowdy people or individuals who possess overly emotional dispositions. Jewish UTFs find it especially sexy when their *goyim* (Yiddish for non-Jewish) mates agree to convert.

Styles Hipsters Avoid

1. **The Goth**—Marilyn Manson and the Trench Coat Mafia put this trend immediately to rest.
2. **The Hippie**—Tie-dyes and patchouli oil became unfashionable when "Touch of Grey" became a hit single.
3. **Rockabilly**—Let's face it—David Lynch is the only person who can pull off the hair. That frado Chris Isaak ruined it for the rest of us.

Goth Is Dead

4. **Village People**—For gay fetishists only, though we still think David Hodo (the construction worker) is deck.
5. **Catholic High School Girl/Cheerleader**—Only cool if you're Asian and even then it's a little creepy. Keep it in the bedroom.
6. **NASA Space Suits**—Popularized by rejects like the Beta Band, this look is definitely one to be avoided.
7. **The Pimp**—Hipsters don't have "bitches" or wear Afro Sheen.
8. **Wiggers**—You're white, dude.
9. **The Steven Seagal**—Ponytails on men are midtown.
10. **The Cyborg**—This probably goes without saying, but if you wear "E-broidery" and sign on to the Internet via a keyboard attached to your shirtsleeve, you need medical attention.

A White Dude with Dreads

11. **Gutter Punks**—You've seen them: dirty, tattooed kids who beg for money. They're just homeless smackheads and are never deck.
12. **White Guys and Girls with Dreadlocks**—Fin.
13. **West Side Story**—This style went out with Fonzie and switchblades, though the switchblade comb is still very fashionable.

14. **The Black Cowboy**—One word—bizarre.

15. **The Europa**—Also known as the Eurotrash look and most commonly associated with black turtlenecks. People will call you Dieter and assume you are a German tourist.

16. **The Kathie Lee**—Pastel dress suits are fin.

17. **The Docker**—An exceptionally unhip and preppy style of dress associated with pleated khakis and brown leather loafers. Commonly found on college campuses known for their "great keggers."

18. **Grunge**—Have patience, grunge is bound to come back. Until then, put your flannel in storage.

19. **Animal Accessorizers**—Nothing is more fin than walking around with a snake, iguana, or ferret around your neck.

20. **Rancid**—Sporting traditional mohawks is for high school kids with ridiculously neglectful and rich, alcoholic parents. This look was never cool outside of London, even in the seventies. Now it's just embarrassing.

Note: Combining two outdated styles like Goth and Catholic High School Girl can be deck.

What About Indie Rockers?

For the past decade, the indie rocker has been integral to the Hipster scene. But categorizing people as indie rockers these days seems a little passé. With the onset of Internet file sharing sources like Limewire and Audiogalaxy, using "indie" as a defining characteristic of the Hipster seems dated.

In the nineties, indie rockers were more than the music they listened to. An entire culture evolved around this unique group. They were a soft-spoken breed prone to wearing undersized T-shirts with

Hipsters Try to Have More Edge These Days

ironic slogans. They considered themselves nerdy and dressed the part. They tended to be pale and thin and were very fond of black glasses with thick plastic rims. They loved Yo La Tengo and Stereolab and were usually in bands themselves.

Indie rock boys had crushes on Asian women who had bodies like fifteen-year-old boys. Indie rock girls liked superskinny boys with unkempt hair. Indie boys prided themselves on being fragile and sickly-looking. Indie women prided themselves on their knee-sock collections and the fact that even *they* were tougher than the average indie rock boy. Both were too shy and awkward to ever make a first move, which might help explain why the breed is dying out.

Needless to say, Hipsters who match this description are everywhere, but the indie movement has become fractured, and people tend to define themselves in more specific terms. Hipsters are now more likely to say they are into a specific style of music like emo or alt-country than to classify themselves as "indie." Characteristics of the indie rocker are still especially prevalent in Loners, WASHes, UTFs, Maxwells, and Polits.

Though icons like Steve Malkmus made being wimpy an attribute, Hipster men today rarely revel in the fact that they are weak, even when they are. They say they are into boxing or begin eating lots of steak to embrace their macho side. Likewise, Hipster women are empowered by their sexuality and have grown tired of dating men who wear Girl Scout T-shirts. Both embrace sleaze culture and know that being PC is for baby boomers and jerries. In general, fans of indie music seem to have a little more edge these days. So, with great fondness, we formally say farewell to the age of the indie rocker.

Hipsters and Non-Hipsters in History: Separating the Deck from the Fin

HOMO ERECTUS (1,750,000–200,000 years ago) Despite the unfortunate name, *Homo erectus* was a very fashionable species. They pioneered the use of tools, actualized utilitarian art, and discovered fire with their mastery of higher reasoning. A little-known fact is that their thick brow ridges and large skulls looked deck in headbands.

Homo Erectus

SAPPHO (circa 630 B.C.) Sappho was a UTF who wrote poetry and taught classes on the isle of Lesbos, an island inhabited solely by women and filled with artists. She wrote deck lesbian lyrics that she sung while strumming a lyre. Even the work of folk masters like Bob Dylan and Gillian Welch pales in comparison to her shit. Sappho didn't create the Hipster archetype, but her life embodied it. Here is a sample of some of her writing, followed by our translation:

To Andromeda

That country girl has witched your wishes,
all dressed up in her country clothes
and she hasn't got the sense
to hitch her rags above her ankles.

Hipster Translation

That redneck tassel dissed you
all dressed up in duds bought at JCPenney
and she's too midtown
to know how to dress deck and stop acting like a chipper.

HOMER (circa 850 B.C.) Homer is midtown. He invented the beauty contest in the *Iliad* writing about a competition between Hera, Athena, and Aphrodite. Zeus was smart enough to refuse to judge, but Paris took the bait and became the first in a long line of pageant hosts such as Bob Barker and Regis Philbin. If Homer were alive today, he'd probably be writing action scripts for Jerry Bruckheimer.

THE TRUNG SISTERS (circa A.D. 40) These deck Vietnamese sisters led a revolution against Chinese fascists and won. They were very punk rock. Legend has it, they were into bondage and had a dominatrix dungeon as well. The first line of an historic poem written about them says it all: "All the male heroes bowed their heads in submission."

JOHN THE BAPTIST (1st century A.D.) J.B. was completely unfashionable, feasted on locusts, and ran about smelling like armpit. In early days, he was a priest of the order of Abia. His job description was to burn incense like a dirty hippie. He was definitely *not* a Hipster. If alive today, he'd be an ex-Deadhead following around Phish and selling pot brownies to make a living. What a jerry.

LAO TZU (6th century B.C.) Lao Tzu is the extraordinarily hip father of Taoism and the author of the *Tao Te Ching*, a favorite religious text for most Hipsters. Many Hipsters (especially UTFs) are fond of the concept of *wu-wei* that he helped pioneer. It instructs one to do nothing: "When nothing is done, nothing is left undone."

CATHERINE DE' MEDICI (1519–1589) A patron of the arts, Catherine de' Medici is considered one of the most influential women of the Renaissance age. She oversaw the construction of a new wing of the Louvre Museum and helped to bring Italian dance to the French by promoting deck parties in the halls of King Louis XIV.

PAUL REVERE (1735–1818) Paul Revere was a Hipster. People are often amazed to find that he never gave a damn about that whole "taxation without representation" thing. He just found the red coats worn by the British to be incredibly tacky. Plus, the tassels all thought Paul was quite a juicer.

SITTING BULL (circa 1831–1890) Sitting Bull loved to chill out. His nickname, Hunkesi, literally means "slow." Though he loved to take it easy, he always managed to kick some cracker ass when he needed to. During one early battle, he walked into enemy fire, sat down, and casually smoked a phatty. He walked away unharmed. He was one deck wally.

GERTRUDE STEIN (1874–1946) Gertrude Stein was a Hipster. She understood the importance of art and loved throwing parties for all the American

Sitting Bull Was Deck

expatriates. Plus, lesbianism is definitely deck unless you have armpit hair, listen to Tori Amos, and go to Lilith.

RAYMOND CHANDLER (1888–1959) Um, he wrote stuff like this: "I was neat, clean, shaved and sober, and I didn't care who knew it."

MATA HARI (1876–1917) Mata Hari was a Hipster. She started her career as a nude dancer, then worked as a spy against the British,

Germans, and French during the First World War. She was executed by firing squad and never revealed who she was working for. Plus she was hot.

MARCEL DUCHAMP (1887–1968) Marcel Duchamp entered a urinal signed "R. Mutt" into an exhibition in 1917. It got rejected, but for six bucks (the price it cost Duchamp to submit the piece) he went into the history books as the founder of conceptual art, and Andy Warhol was provided a career. Duchamp was the quintessential Hipster.

e. e. cummings (1894–1962) The best poet to ever walk on earth, cummings is deified by all Hipsters, even if he did write for *Vanity Fair*. Writing your name in lowercase is deck, so despite what the E. E. Cummings Society has to say about it, we'll continue to spell it correctly.

AMELIA EARHART (1898–1937) Sure, she was the first woman to fly across the Atlantic, showing the world that women are as capable as men of accomplishing their dreams, but personally we just think women who wear aviation hats and goggles are deck.

MARLENE DIETRICH (1901–1992) The Berlin-born vamp Marlene Dietrich had more attitude than a pit bull beaten with a cat. The hedonistic star of *Blonde Venus* got liquid with countless suitors of both genders, often performed in drag, was known to throw back a beer or two with Hemingway, and even inspired the deck song "Lola" by the Kinks.

CLARK GABLE (1901–1960) Clark Gable was a frado. That mustache was simply unforgivable. Plus, he helped spawn Burt Reynolds and Tom Selleck, two other embarrassing frados.

CAB CALLOWAY (1907–1994) Known as "the man in the zoot suit with the reet pleats," Cab Calloway is a Hipster icon. He was an uninhibited and outrageous bandleader who often headlined the Cotton Club, and his tunes "Reefer Man" and "Minnie the Moocher" are timeless classics. Calloway single-handedly introduced the lingo of the streets to the world.

JACQUES COUSTEAU (1910–1997) He helped develop the Aqua-Lung, was a spy during World War II, and created the Cousteau Society to protect our seas, all in addition to bringing those deck underwater shows to TV. Nobody is cooler.

YUL BRYNNER (1915–1985) Yul made baldness chic. At the onset of his career he played guitar in nightclubs with Russian Gypsies, had a trapeze act, and schmoozed with Jean Cocteau. Later, he looked deck adorning Egyptian pharaoh duds on the big screen, a difficult task for most to pull off. His coolness depreciated substantially after endless touring as the star of *The King and I*, but Yul Brynner is nevertheless remembered fondly by Hipsters.

BIRD (1920–1955) Bird gave birth to cool before it was deck. His music remains hip, despite the embarrassing gushing of nerds like Ken Burns. He is also the NBA's 12th all-time leading scorer and was an invaluable asset to the Celtics.

JACK KEROUAC (1922–1969) The poster boy of Hipsters. No explanation needed.

JACQUELINE KENNEDY ONASSIS (1929–1994) Thank God no one assassinated Jackie-O. The tassels would still be dressing like June Cleaver.

BOB ROSS (1931–1995) Sadly, Bob became part of history prematurely when he passed away at the young age of fifty-two. Thankfully, we can still catch him painting "happy" trees, rivers, and mountains on PBS and marvel at his eminently cool afro.

BOZO THE CLOWN (PRE–WILLARD SCOTT) (1946–1960) Bozo was an original wally. He wore punk red hair in 1946, knew how to keep the kids in check, and never let Cookie lead the Grand

March. Willard Scott assumed the role in the early 1960s and did irreparable damage to the Bozo name. Incidentally, Scott donned a Ronald McDonald suit around the same time.

Choosing a Look

Rockabilly:

Is This Style Deck or Fin?

Answer: This style is fin.

HIPSTER PERSONALITY TYPE:

The Clubber

- - - - - - - - - - -

Definition: Younger Hipsters from the Gen-Y set who love to dance, listen to electronic music, and promote parties.

Question: Are you a Hipster?
Answer: Why categorize people? When you are on E and the bass is thumping, everyone is beautiful.

- - - - - - - - - - -

ATTIRE/PRESENTATION

Today's Clubber is easily spotted in a crowd. Just be on the lookout for the baggy pants, thick-soled sneaks, and the glitter around their eyes. They wear T-shirts with cartoon drawings and Japanese decals and often put shiny stickers on their faces. Clubbers accessorize with designer water bottles, gold teeth caps, wristbands, and sometimes even Pop Rocks. In the nineties, Clubbers sucked on baby pacifiers to keep from grinding their teeth when on E. Clubbers today are edgier and grind at will.

BACKGROUND AND UPBRINGING

Clubbers generally have middle- to upper-middle-class upbringings and generally come of age in suburbs in close proximity to cities. Most are pretty fin, but we'll cut them some slack because they are young and often provide good drugs for other Hipsters.

PHILOSOPHY

Hugging is deck. In many ways, Clubbers have taken their cue from hippie culture, adopting a communal "love your neighbor" vibe at their parties. Dancing-bear T-shirts have been replaced by Powerpuff Girl belly shirts, but all the elements of drugs, dancing, peace, and love remain the same.

AVERSION

Curfews.

DISPOSITION

Impressionable. Clubbers believe whatever you tell them and are easy to steal from.

THE HOME

Many Clubbers are in their teens and still live at home with their parents. Older Clubbers take up residence at Betty Ford.

EDUCATION AND CAREER

Since most Clubbers are of the younger Gen-Y set, they don't have careers and simply work at the supermarket. More rebellious Clubbers sell E. Older Clubbers are usually too tired to dance until dawn and become Neo-Crunches. Clubbers have professional interests in fashion design, printmaking, audio production, and pharmaceuticals. As per education, most claim to have "street knowledge" even if they grew up on Deer Creek Drive.

MODE OF TRAVEL

Dad's car, walking.

WARNING

They are probably too young to have sex with.

TRIBAL CLUBBERS

Some Clubbers form their own exclusive tribes and throw smaller, unannounced parties to keep away the gutter punks and cops who crash larger events. Tribal Clubbers call one another family and create acronyms for their tribes, such as IBM (International Beat Masons).

Some tribes adopt a drug-free, straight-edge lifestyle and tattoo X's on their hands, but this is somewhat uncommon. Tribal Clubbers prefer smaller parties where they know nobody will steal their Mad Libs books out of their backpacks.

MUSIC AND PARTIES

The Clubber listens exclusively to mix CDs and compilations with titles like *Chill Out Volume 26* and *Deep Trance from Germany, Volume 4*. They spend a great deal of time at record-store listening bars checking out the latest dance music and trying to keep their pants from falling past their knees.

Though Clubbers will always enjoy dancing until dawn at parties and clubs (the term "rave" is only used by nerdy newsmagazine shows like *Dateline*), the booming bass of jungle and house music has given way to so-called "IDM" (intelligent dance music). This type of electronic music is darker than the happy-go-lucky house music of the nineties that was spun by DJs with names like DJ Mega or DJ Sunshine Belt. Currently, DJs have dropped the title "DJ" and prefer names such as "Loco" and "InterPlanetaryBeatSex." Attaching "DJ" to your name is very nineties.

DATING A CLUBBER

Common Turn-ons—Hello Kitty or Badtz Maru bedsheets, sitting Indian style, applying henna tattoos, strobe lights, fake IDs

Major Turnoff—Doc Martens

Clubbers fall in and out of love with the change of each season and enjoy dating people who possess a buoyant attitude and a lightness of spirit. They enjoy socializing in large groups, and if you can offer up a group of multicultural friends as a dating dowry, you will be a hit. Make the Clubber a good mix tape and always be sure to look deck on the dance floor. Don't say you like Moby or Sasha and Digweed when asked what music you prefer, and never use the term "electronica." Clubbers enjoy talking about astrology, and, if it's in the stars, they'll let you get liquid with them in the bathroom while they're peaking.

Dining, Diet, and Dinner Parties

Choosing a Place to Gluten

Hipsters have very refined tastes when it comes to food and drink. They never dine at chains like Applebee's and T.G.I. Friday's. If pictures of the dishes are on the menu, Hipsters will generally avoid the establishment. If the waitstaff is wearing suspenders, name tags, or matching plaid aprons, Hipsters will definitely stay away. Places that serve wings or poppers are midtown. Nevertheless, meals *can* be ironic, and Hipsters occasionally throw their rules out the door to enjoy a kitschy dinner at Denny's or Big Boy.

Hipsters go to restaurants incessantly and often spend more time deciding where to eat than eating itself. They prefer restaurants that write their menus on chalkboards, have low ceilings, use soft lighting, and have waiters with body odor. When there is a musky waitstaff, Hipsters feel confident the food will be authentic.

Hipsters also believe that having to wait awhile for one's table is essential to the overall dining experience. This gives them the opportunity to check out the vibe and show off their outfits. If Hipsters are seated immediately, they will become uncomfortable, shift tensely in their chairs, and most assuredly not enjoy their meal.

Vegetarians and Carnivores

It's common knowledge that a good percentage of Hipsters are vegans and vegetarians. This is especially true of Neo-Crunches, Clubbers, Polits, and even some Loners. These personality types tend to be advocates of animal rights and environmental causes. To them, eating meat is suburban. Others, known as Enigmatards, adhere to a strict no-meat-or-dairy philosophy in their diet, but wear lots of leather.

Lately, many Hipsters have become devout carnivores who take great pride in a meat-heavy diet. They eat burgers and meat on the bone to demonstrate how in touch they are with their "tribal" selves. This type of Hipster often reads a lot of Bukowski and plans weekend getaways to the dog track.

When ordering red meat at a restaurant, the Hipster should always make sure it is cooked rare or medium-rare. Ordering a well-cooked burger is like calling the waitress "toots": something you simply don't do. Part of the splendor of eating a tasty slab of red meat is being able to see a little blood. More analytical Hipsters think preferring to "see a little pink in your meat" has Freudian implications and debate this theory while waiting for the meal to arrive.

The Kitschy Dinner Party

Hipsters love inviting their friends over for dinner and frequently try to outkitsch one another when preparing a meal. Here are some popular props and dishes that are staples at Hipster dinner parties.

Favorite kitschy dinner party props:

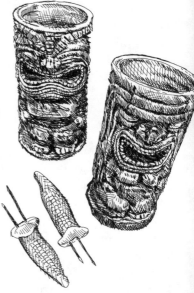

- Red-and-white checkerboard table-cloth
- Decorative corn-on-the-cob holders
- An apron that says "*Martha Stewart Living*" or "Kiss the Chef"
- Tiki-style cocktail glasses
- Mitten pot holders that say "Aloha"
- Frankenstein and Bride of Frankenstein salt and pepper shakers
- After-dinner mints
- Melmac salad bowl set
- Crocheted doilies
- Smoking jackets

Favorite kitschy dinner party meals:

- TV Dinners
- Chipped Beef on White Bread (chipped seiten can substitute)
- Casseroles
- Fondue
- Sloppy Joes
- Baby Back Ribs
- Macaroni and Cheese
- Meatloaf
- Schlitz-battered fish
- Frozen pizza with Tater Tots

Choosing a Look

The John Deere:

Is This Style Deck or Fin?

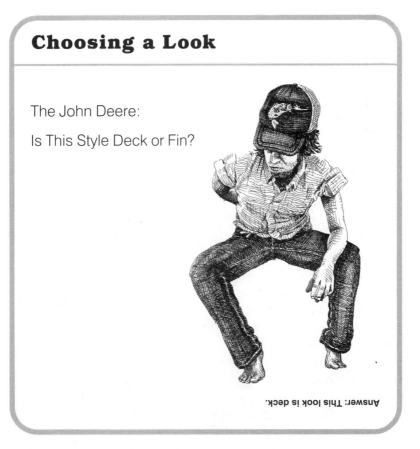

Answer: This look is deck.

The Loner

Definition: Introverted Hipsters who have little time for social engagements due to a borderline obsessive relationship with their hobbies and/or work. Loners have anal-retentive tendencies, collect music compulsively, and feel awkward socially.

Question: Are you a Hipster?
Answer: I have a large collection of obscure Belgian techno mastermixes on limited edition vinyl. That's pretty deck, right?

ATTIRE/PRESENTATION

Loners are usually very pale and thin and straddle the line between deck and dweeb. The Loner can immediately cross over to the latter when his/her hair becomes overly greasy, and must be wary of this fact. The Loner male usually wears Elvis Costello–style glasses, and the Loner female is a big fan of horned rims. Loners who don't need glasses often wear them anyway.

BACKGROUND AND UPBRINGING

Loners come from middle-class backgrounds and come of age in suburbs exclusively. Since they spend most of their formative years acquiring pop culture knowledge watching television, it can be said that they are home-schoolers. Most have nicknames like "Faggot" or "Dirt-Dog" in high school and move to cities as soon as they can.

PHILOSOPHY
Hypochondria is deck.

AVERSION
Records with scratches.

DISPOSITION
Self-deprecating. Loners know that a little self-loathing can be charming and use this to their full advantage, saying things like, "This is the first time in three weeks I've gone out on a weekend; I'm so lame." Loners tend to be introverted and keep emotional attachments at arm's length. Loners enjoy spending time with friends, but are usually too consumed with their own projects to sustain multiple relationships. They tend to flinch when they hear loud noises.

THE HOME
Loners are pack rats who never throw anything away. They accumulate too many possessions to make moving practical and tend to remain in the same apartment for years. It would not be unusual for the Loner to hold on to his/her Intellivision game cartridges from the eighties, even though the player has been broken for a decade.

Female Loners are often into feng shui. They infuriate roommates by reassembling their settings every few weeks to achieve perfect harmony with their environment. People who live with them may find the refrigerator in one of the bedrooms, if Loners deem that space the "digestive corner." These types of idiosyncrasies make it easiest for Loners to live alone.

EDUCATION AND CAREER
Most Loners attend colleges where indie rock T-shirts and geek chic are fashionable. They never attend colleges that are Greek. Many Loners choose careers in programming, video editing, and other technical skills. Others work in libraries and bookstores, and sometimes for Kinko's. All Loners enjoy work that allows them to organize and alphabetize things. Despite their notoriously bushy or oily hairdos, they have a penchant for organization, provided they aren't stoned.

MODES OF TRAVEL
Pintos and Oldsmobiles, walking.

DWEEB TENDENCIES
A large portion of Loners are interested in computers and programming. Too avid an interest in computers can quickly depreciate the Hipster status of the Loner. Spending too much time in chat rooms, programming viruses, and arguing that Telnet is superior to e-mail is never fashionable. Similarly, T-shirts with slogans like "Programming is not a crime" or with anti-Microsoft rhetoric are fin.

Loners are often genre-ists. They are usually into sci-fi, film noir, comics, and horror movies. No true Hipster would ever go to a Star Trek convention, but Loners have plenty of friends from high school who try to convince them that maybe they should. The urge is there, but the Loner knows that not acting on this and similar desires is what keeps him or her from becoming a dweeb. Battling impulses such as these is a daily struggle for the Loner.

DATING A LONER

Common Turn-ons—mix tapes, black socks with shorts, bitten nails, peeling skin, an aversion to sports, a fondness for cats

Major Turnoff—confidence

If you are trying to impress a Loner, we recommend being self-deprecating. They don't seek out depressed or insecure partners, but they do appreciate a partner who has a whimsical sense of humor about him/herself. Loners enjoy the company of someone who prefers a quiet night at home. They fancy independent partners who don't want to sleep over constantly. Some Loners sign onto makeouclub.com with names like emo_lover23 to find a date, but if you are too computer savvy or know how to speak Klingon, you will blow your chances with them. On second dates, Loners are prone to testing the temperature of the relationship by watching a favorite movie or playing a cherished record. Be aware that this is usually a test that you can only pass or fail.

The Cosmopolitan Cosmopolitan: Choosing a Bar

Hipsters are notorious barflies who spend more time relaxing and socializing than the average person. Not surprisingly, they are very selective about where they drink. Franchises and chains are routinely avoided, and the Hipster wouldn't be caught dead in a place like Coyote Ugly. If bleached-blonde tassels are dancing on the countertops, pouring cheap liquor down the throats of suits and frat boys, Hipsters will run and not look back.

Sports Bars Are Midtown

Dodging the Neon: Knowing Which Bars to Avoid

- **Sports Bars**—Jocks who wear numbered jerseys or white baseball caps and stand around yelling at TV monitors are never Hipsters. Hipster women receive unwanted advances in such environments, and some varieties of Hipsters (especially Polits, Loners, and Glam Rockers) put their lives in jeopardy when entering a sports bar.

- **Bars with Dartboards**—Bars that have dartboards tend to attract the same crowds found at sports bars. Hipsters know that people who play darts are usually date rapists and are never deck. They prefer pool, foosball, pinball, and Ms. Pac-Man.

- **Bars with Blended Drinks**—Bars that sell Bahama mamas, daiquiris, piña coladas, and other blended drinks containing coconut rum are not Hipster favorites. These bars draw in boys who like Jimmy Buffett and the type of women one sees on the E! channel.

- **Cigar Bars**—Cigar bars are frequented by creepy CEOs and Wall Street types who shred questionable accounting documents and cheat on their wives with hookers. They always smell like sulfur, which is appropriate, since Hipsters consider cigar bars to be the lowest chamber of hell.

- **High-Profile Bars and Clubs**—Bars with beefy bouncers and stretch limos parked outside are midtown. They attract the fashion-deprived elite and are almost always tourist traps for Hipster wanna-bes, guys with ponytails, and tassels with flubber. Plus, Hipsters never want to be photographed by paparazzi.

Another Round, Please:
Bars Frequented by Hipsters

- **The Dive**—Dives are always dark and musty and attract a handful of red-nosed locals who have been frequenting the establishment for decades. They emanate a stale-booze-and-cigarette stench that is tantalizing to most Hipsters. A good dive bar has Sinatra on the jukebox as well as compilations of truckers' greatest hits, like "Coal Miner's Daughter."

    When at a dive, Hipsters are willing to overlook lapses in judgment that would be inexcusable elsewhere. For instance, Hipsters would never drink domestic beer from a tap, but at a dive bar this can be very deck. Though most Hipsters avoid speaking to the locals, conforming to their customs is keeping it real and edgy. Plus, one should never rock the boat when at a dive. The owner's brother may show up and kick your ass.

- **The Lounge**—Lounges are Hipster bars decorated with asymmetrical couches, easy chairs, and sofas made of velvet. Candles, fireplaces, and kitschy lamps from the sixties and seventies are the lighting of choice. Lounges are ideal for philosophical or seductive banter while sharing a mojito and a one-hitter. The music is smooth and melodic. Hipsters who say things like "I'm metal as fuck" or "Wiccans are gay" rarely go to lounges.

- **The Beat**—Beats are Hipster dance clubs with monosyllabic names like Bob, Shine, and Plant. Since most dance clubs are pretty fin, beats must distinguish themselves from other run-of-the-mill establishments. First, they tend to have smaller dance floors with lower ceilings. Enormous clubs with pounding techno attract girls who wear hair spray and piss off the DJ by requesting "Who Let the Dogs Out?" Secondly, beats never spin gay house or disco. Instead, Hipsters groove out to electroclash, hip-hop, trance, and similar types of music. Hipster women are especially fond of beats since they can avoid unwanted grinding from creepy men with semis. Some beats, known as **lounge beats,** combine these two bar types by providing a chill-out environment with a tiny dance floor.

- **The Neo-Dive**—Neo-dives are bars owned by Hipsters (usually older WASHes or UTFs) that are designed and decorated to give the illusion of age. Neo-dives have either a pool table or a retro video game like Ms. Pac-Man, Joust, or Destroyer. The owners let the grime tastefully accumulate to give the establishment a classic feel.

Neo-dives are exclusive Elks clubs for Hipsters. Non-Hipsters who stumble into them may hear Hipsters grumbling things like, "I didn't know Amway was in town," or, "The Sugar Ray concert must have just ended."

Choosing a Look

The Gutter Punk:

Is This Style

Deck or Fin?

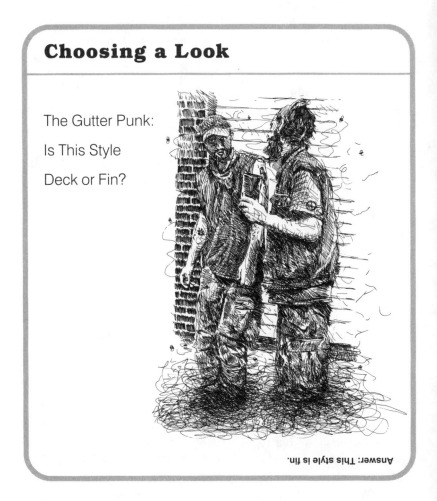

Answer: This style is fin.

The Perfect Bronson

- **Imports and Microbrews**—Wise choices for the connoisseur. Imported beers such as Guinness and microbrews from small independent breweries are the beers of choice for Hipsters.
- **Budweiser**—A classic beer enjoyed by all Hipsters, especially those who wear John Deere mesh caps. Drinking Budweiser while bitching about Gap ads and corporate America can make you seem mysterious rather than hypocritical.
- **PBR**—The best-tasting domestic beer. Very popular with guys in work shirts and cowgirl Hipsters. The one beer that is cool to drink out of a can.
- **Schlitz**—Schlitz may be the only thing cool about Wisconsin, the state that brought us the cheesehead hat.
- **Michelob**—For when you are feeling as smooth as Billy Dee. Offer to buy someone a Michelob and he/she will know you want to get jiggy.
- **Mickey's Big Mouth**—The only deck malt liquor. The hornet logo makes a great tattoo for the more savvy Mickey's fan. The old-school, pull-off tabs are greatly missed.
- **Miller High Life**—A good beer to drink when feeling nostalgic, since you probably used to steal them from your old man.
- **Zima**—Ignore the naysayers. Drinking Zima is deck.

Finely Brewed for Greasers:
Beers Hipsters Avoid

- All light beers
- Coors
- Busch
- Tequiza
- Rolling Rock
- Milwaukee's Best
- Malt liquor (excluding Mickey's)
- Ice beers

Deck Chowder: Hipster Cocktails

- **Cosmopolitan, Martini, Manhattan**—The holy trinity for Hipsters. Some are fond of saying things like, "Manhattans are totally nineties," but they are dumbasses.
- **Mai Tai**—A kitschy cocktail that will make you feel like a drunk, middle-aged femme fatale begging for some steamy afternoon delight.
- **Tequila Sunrise**—When made with a golden tequila and some fresh-squeezed OJ, nothing is more deck. But be careful, the whole aesthetic can be ruined if the bartender stirs the grenadine "sunrise" out of the bottom of the glass. Also, Tang is never an acceptable substitute for orange juice.
- **Scotch on the Rocks**—Simple, classic. A fine scotch drunk from a heavy rocks glass will make you feel like royalty. Best consumed in a dark, wood-paneled room while sitting in a leather chair.
- **Bloody Mary**—The quintessential brunch cocktail. Note: Asking the waitress for a BM is midtown.
- **Maker's Mark and Coke**—Though Jim Beam and Jack Daniel's are midtown, nothing is classier than the smooth, distinct flavor of Maker's Mark, the true Hipster whiskey. And no, they didn't pay us to say that.
- **Mojito**—A new favorite. Unfortunately, when they aren't made with fresh mint and lime, mojitos taste like ass.
- **Caipirinhas**—This drink is way too sweet. Luckily, nobody stocks cachaça, so you'll sound cool ordering it but won't get stuck with a lame cocktail.

Midtown Happy Hour:
Cocktails Hipsters Avoid

- Green apple martini
- Long Island iced tea
- Drinks with suggestive names
- Bahama mamas
- Shooters
- Gin and juice
- Zombies
- Drinks that have to be set on fire
- Fuzzy navels and other schnapps drinks
- Jägermeister

Gotta Light? Hipster Cigarettes

- **Gauloise**—The cigarette to smoke when feeling arty.
- **American Spirit**—When you are feeling healthy and/or anti-corporate.
- **Camels**—The most popular Hipster cigarette. Camels spelled with a K are popular with Clubbers who buy anything with the letter K on it, given their fondness for horse tranquilizers.
- **Lucky Strike**—Best to smoke when you are feeling tough and want to appear blue-collar.
- **Drum**—For Hipsters in denial, who say they smoke less if they roll their own.
  - **Imported brands you've never heard of**—Smoked by Hipsters who aren't really smokers but want a cool accessory.
  - **Newport**—Makes your phlegm minty!
  - **Capri**—Not for the serious smoker, but they make great props.
  - **Marlboro Lights**—Totally midtown and should be avoided. Note: If you are a woman, Marlboro Lights (a.k.a. slut butts) are especially suspicious.

HIPSTER PERSONALITY TYPE:

The Schmooze

Definition: Networking Hipsters obsessed with their careers. Schmoozes are sometimes known as "Hipster lite" because they flaunt their Hipster status to secure a better job.

Question: Are you a Hipster?
Answer: Hold on one second; you say this book is going to be published by Random House? My friend Andrew is an editor there. Do you know him?

ATTIRE/PRESENTATION

Schmoozes dress for success, wearing eighties-style smart casual and accessorizing with vintage brooches, decorative totes, big sunglasses, showy belt buckles, and occasionally eye-catching platinum pimp rings. The Schmooze's favorite designer is Helmut Lang, and he/she tends to work out to maintain a firm body. They never wear sneakers. Male Schmoozes who have ponytails are cheesy.

BACKGROUND AND UPBRINGING

Schmoozes often grow up in suburbs on the fringes of New York, L.A., Chicago, and D.C. In many ways they are the opposite of

UTFs, since they try to create the illusion of status, even if they have to do so on credit. Many grow up across the street from UTFs and become overachievers to compete with them. Some Schmoozes had parents who walked around the house naked or threw swingers parties. To avoid seeing them naked, they locked themselves in their rooms, studying and planning ways to be financially independent.

PHILOSOPHY AND BELIEFS
Whatever they read in hidden self-help books.
Going to a therapist is very fashionable.
If you are useful to a Schmooze, *your* philosophy and beliefs.

AVERSION
Chewing tobacco.

DISPOSITION
Trendy and/or pretentious. Schmoozes frequent bars that decorate with ferns and mirrors, buy clothing based upon the designer, and smoke French cigarettes pulled elegantly from monogrammed silver holders. When attending social events, Schmoozes strategically place themselves in close proximity to those seen as being useful. They speak loudly and often incorrectly on a wide range of topics including art nouveau, video installations, linguistics, and philosophy. They scour art-history books to find useful terms like "occidentalism."

THE HOME
Schmoozes tend to buy framed prints of more obvious artists such as Edward Hopper and Chagall. Many have glass-top coffee tables that are conducive to doing coke. When embarrassed by a surplus of IKEA furniture in their homes, they claim they are being postmodern.

EDUCATION AND CAREER
Schmoozes attend public and private colleges alike, and all try to excel in their departments. They generally have jobs as production assistants early in their careers. The Schmooze's ultimate goal is a power job in a creative industry, and in order to infiltrate the scene they realize that they must become hip themselves by reading the right books, wearing the best clothing, and attending the deckest parties.

Finding socially acceptable ways to "Darwin the scene," as they call it, is important to their agendas. One example is asking strangers at parties what they do for a living and following this up with a pointed, "And where did you go to college?" for good measure. Asking these simple questions is the easiest way for the Schmooze to separate the strong from the weak. They surround themselves with the well-to-do and have intense eye-contact skills. Looking away while speaking to someone is a sign of weakness, so they often carry eyedrops to stay in top form.

FAVORITE MODE OF TRAVEL
BMWs, Vespas, vintage convertibles.

MISCELLANEOUS
Schmoozes never drink beer. Instead, they prefer martinis, mojitos, Manhattans, and red wine. Always consistent in pretension, Schmoozes tend to end their e-mails and letters with a flip "Cheers," regardless of whether they are British. They have a limited interest in culture, fashion, music, and art in comparison to other Hipsters and tend to like borderline-hip bands like Outkast. Regardless of their upbringing, Schmoozes often turn to Buddhism in their twenties and use the word "Zen" whenever the opportunity arises.

SUBCATEGORIES OF THE SCHMOOZE
- **Name-Dropping Star Fucker** (NDSF)—This form of Schmooze often drops the names of *Page Six* stars at social events in order to impress. The NDSF will often try to insinuate that he/she has slept with a famous celebrity, knowing that having a Gwyneth or a Toby as a notch on the belt instantly improves one's status.
- **The Actual** (pronounced **act**-choo-owl)—a Schmooze who has actually befriended or slept with a notable celebrity.

WARNING
One should be wary not to invite too many Schmoozes to a social event. They are exceptionally competitive and have been known to spill drinks upon one another to prompt a departure. A small portion of Schmoozes are dangerous pathological liars prone to fits of rage.

ACCENTS SCHMOOZES MAY ADOPT TO ENHANCE THEIR SOCIAL PRESENCE

- French—when trying to get someone in bed
- German—when attending an art opening
- British—when applying for a job
- Australian—by mistake when drunk
- Southern—to appear quaint
- Ebonic—to give a little edge
- Staten Island—never

DATING A SCHMOOZE

Common Turn-ons—submissive types with bad posture who enjoy doing laundry, shoplifting, business cards dipped in fine perfume, clean underwear, quickies

Major Turnoff—fanzines

The Schmooze is very selective when picking a mate. In fact, Schmoozes generally prefer being single, since bringing a date to social engagements can curtail their efforts to appeal to the libidos of power players. Plus, many Schmoozes are overachievers who feel they don't have time to date. To attract Schmoozes, appeal to their desire to succeed, whisper sweet nothings in their ear, and tell them that the "honors" section of their résumé makes you hot. Though Schmoozes enjoy brief and fully physical affairs, the easiest way to win the heart of a Schmooze is by showing that you are a force to be reckoned with yourself. Otherwise, they will be happy to dominate the relationship or to simply love you and leave you.

Hipster Grooming:
More Than a Matter of Style

Facial Hair

Facial hair (or the lack thereof) is rarely a simple choice for Hipsters. In fact, the looks they choose for themselves can illustrate a multitude of things about their personalities. Many Hipsters choose to wear the same style as the lead singer of their favorite band. Whether this is a conscious or subconscious decision is open for debate. For others, a more complex psychology is involved. Here are some common facial hair choices and what they communicate:

- **The Standard 'Stache**—Generally worn by Hipsters who have recently seen a slide show where their dad looked pretty cool during the sixties or seventies with a mustache. Though mustaches can be extremely deck, Hipsters should limit wearing one to no longer than four months at a time, at which point the kitsch factor becomes tiresome.

- **The Handlebar Mustache**—Worn by Hipsters who have watched too much porn. Despite its seedy origin, the handlebar mustache can add an element of kitsch to the right cronkite. Gay men should avoid the handlebar unless they want to look slutty or like one of the Village People.

- **The John Waters**—Unless you're trying to cash a check with John Waters's name on it, avoid this style at all costs. Even John Waters looks foolish. Ditto for Dali-style mustaches.

- **Chops**—Hipsters with chops are laid-back jokesters. They tend to have a chops-wearing hero, like Elvis or Captain Beefheart, whose style they love to emulate. Hipsters who have chops should avoid hanging out together, since they will look like those couples who wear matching warm-up suits.

- **Indie Burns**—Adorned by most Hipster males, indie burns are a classic Hipster fashion style. For those who harvest lighter crops of hair on their faces, indie burns will appear disturbingly pubescent.

- **Full Beard**—With the exception of Neo-Crunches, who grow full beards because they are too lazy to shave, the full beard on the Hipster signifies a desire to be taken seriously as an artist or thinker. The full beard communicates that one is too concerned with the profundity of life to be distracted by trivial shaving rituals. When a Hipster grows a full beard, he has entered his "blue period," a more reflective and serious phase.

- **Traditional Goatee**—Having a goatee is like setting the thermostat to seventy-two degrees. It's the perfect style for almost anyone. If your look has become too preppy, a goatee will add just the right amount of edge to your appearance. Likewise, if your beard has become too unkempt and you look like a biker, trimming things back a tad can keep you from looking like a greaser.

- **Pencil-line Beard and Goatee**—A popular look for wiggers and people who think Jay-Z is cool. This look is fin.

- **Devil Beard**—Wooooo, I'm frightened of the big scary man with the pointed beard. Let's get out of here quickly; he's so subversive. Run! Run like the wind!

- **Perma-Shadow**—Worn by guys who are in the closet. Women never enjoy the scratchiness of a man's face when he neglects to shave for a couple of days, and Hipsters who adorn this look consistently are happy to keep them at bay. Don Johnson and George Michael ruined this look for everyone.

- **Urban Amish**—Uncommon and worn exclusively by Bipsters, Teeters, and WASHes. Hipsters with the Urban Amish look listen to guitar-driven music and really dig Slayer. It's a useful style for Hipsters who want to pretend they are badasses.

- **Chin Shrub**—Worn by enigmatic types who want to "mess with your mind." They raise the question, Is this a beard or is it something else altogether? They are fond of saying things like, "Nobody *really* knows anyone else," and often point to their chin shrubs to illustrate how things in life are never black-and-white.

- **The Divot**—For the more agreeable Hipster. Gives the illusion that your bottom lip is pursed, an expression that Bill Clinton made famous. Hipsters who adorn the divot put everyone around them at ease and often use this to their advantage.

Follicles, Pores, and Flubber: Grooming, Makeup, and Surgery for the Hipster Female

- **Eyebrows**—When it comes to maintaining one's eyebrows, the decision to wax, pluck, or go au naturel is largely up to the individual. Painted eyebrows are always midtown, but otherwise Hipsters have a wide range of choice. An interesting fact is that all Loners are pluckers. Loners who smoke too much pot have been known to go overboard with the tweezers while sitting in front of the TV. They grow their bangs long to compensate for overzealous plucking.

- **Legs/Armpits**—One of the more famous looks for the Hipster female is the **Hairy Armpit–Smooth Legs Dichotomy (HASLD).** To pull this style off it is imperative that a tank top and skirt be worn; otherwise your efforts will be in vain. This look informs the casual observer that you have a sense of irony and that even though you've traveled Europe and adopted their unshaven ways beneath the arms, you still respect the good American value of baby-smooth legs. When not paired with silky, hair-free legs, underarm hair is a fashion faux pas. Without exception, leg hair is for jerries.

- **Bikini Lines**—Hipsters are fairly diverse when it comes to choosing a grooming style for their bikini lines. Brazilian Bikini Waxes that leave a finger-length vertical stripe in front, can be the perfect decision for Hipsters who want to add a little irony to their vaginas. Similar to handlebar moustaches on men, Brazilian Bikini Waxes are kitschy and should be worn

Sculpting Hearts Is Fin

only for a short duration. Removing all hair, Playboy-style, is a waste of time since Hipsters never wear thong bikinis. Many Hipsters let things grow naturally and brag that their vaginas are "old school."

- **Botox, Plastic Surgery, Implants**—Popular surgical procedures in Miami and L.A., but Hipsters don't live in these places.

Excuse Me While I Powder My Nose Ring: Hipster Makeup

Most Hipsters opt for simplicity when it comes to makeup and choose to simply go without. They believe that wearing makeup outside of weddings is bourgeois. No Hipster would ever pull out a vanity mirror in public and begin applying Revlon, but when worn smartly, makeup can be very fashionable. Here are some popular (and unpopular) Hipster makeup styles and their corresponding meanings:

- **Foundation**—Worn by anchorwomen, sorority girls, and by women who deify Susan Lucci. Hipsters never wear foundation.
- **Blush**—see *Foundation.*
- **Black and Plum Lipstick**—Dark lipstick says "back off." Girls who have grown tired of advances by cheesy guys know that wearing a little black lipstick will keep frat boys and Wall Street types at arm's length. Perfect for Hipsters into punk and electroclash music.
- **Red and Pink Lipstick**—Red lipstick can communicate that you are into postfeminism and know that you are a fine-looking tassel. Smearing a little across one's face can be a nice touch for Hipsters who adorn torn prom dresses. Note: Leaving a little on a coffee mug, a cigarette, or a friend's cheek can be fashionably retro.
- **Face Powdering**—Unless we enter another Victorian age, this look has been retired. Fair complexions are always attractive, but why look like Nosferatu?
- **Glitter and Body Shimmer**—Adorning oneself with glitter and/ or body shimmer is an especially popular look for the Clubber. If you want to purchase some E, but don't want to approach

strangers, wearing glitter is a sure way to attract them. Note: Glitter and body shimmer are flashy and playful on the weekend, but should not be worn to work.

- **Dark Blue or Black Eyeliner (heavily applied)**—Dark eyeliner is most often worn by Hipsters who are feeling impulsive. When worn by Neo-Crunches, Loners, Polits, and Clubbers, however, dark eyeliner can indicate feelings of isolation or depression.

- **Racoon Eyes**—A heavy coat of dark eye makeup surrounding the eyes signifies that the Hipster is feeling reflective, and perhaps embarking upon an artistic stage marked by profound inner searching. Darkening one's eyes "to be more like Gwyneth," who looked deck in *The Royal Tenenbaums*, is kinda silly.

Hipster Hairdos for Men

Pomo Pomp

Grizzow

Emo Combover

Neo Panther

Mulletude

Northern Pull

Faux Hawk

Business Jiggy

Casablanca

Tossed Caesar

Chiadome

Jewfro

Hipster Hairdos for Women

Fluxus

Wet Banana

Wispy Dixie

Bouvier

Electromullet

Peg Boy

Barely Legal

Uncle Eddie

Skunk Nugs

Ratt's Nest

B. Toklas

Speedway

55

Maxwells, Carpets,

and CK-1s

Definition: Gay, lesbian, and bisexual Hipsters who are *aggressively* open about their sexuality. (Note: Gay and bisexual Hipsters who are more under-stated about their sexuality commonly fit into other categories.)

Question: Are you a Hipster?
Answer: Who's more fabulous than me? Being straight is gay!

Maxwells

There are 2 different types of Maxwells, known as the **Formfitting Maxwell** and the **Glam Rocker**. Both types of Maxwells differentiate themselves from other gay males by not listening to house or music by "divas." Maxwells never snap their fingers or say, "You go, girlfriend." They mix well with all Hipster personality types and avoid solely gay bars and gyms. Maxwells also steer clear of gay men with embarrassing names like Sharkey or Fabian.

A Formfitting Maxwell

ATTIRE/PRESENTATION

Glam Rockers generally wear a little rouge on their cheeks, mesh shirts, and skintight leather pants. They try to illuminate their presence with an entourage of stylishly dressed ladies. Formfitting Maxwells are known for their impeccable fashion sense. They shop in the finest stores and purchase the latest Prada and Diesel wear. Both avoid the frat-boy look, the warm-up–suit look, and most important, Goth.

PHILOSOPHY AND BELIEFS
FFM—Going out for juice can be a nice break from going to a bar.
Glam Rocker—"I'm the biggest fairy in this town so don't fuck with me."

DISPOSITION
FFM—aloof.
Glam Rocker—dandy.

AVERSION
FFM—used clothing, spitting.
Glam Rocker—people who dance with the white-man overbite, denim.

SEX
FFM—bottom in the early stages, top when in love.
Glam Rocker—bottom.

**WISEST DECISION TO MAKE IF ENTERING
A SPORTS BAR MISTAKENLY**
FFM—Pretend to be the busboy, then sneak out the bathroom window.
Glam Rocker—Run.

Carpets

Like Maxwells, Carpets can similarly be broken down into two major subcategories, the **Metal Carpet** and the **Plush Carpet.** Metal and Plush Carpets both instinctively avoid clichés associated with lesbian culture. As any Hipster knows, the Indigo Girls and other sentimental girlie-folk sucks, and trying to cloak your femininity is lilith.

ATTIRE/PRESENTATION
Metal Carpets are Hipsters who tend to like metal and punk. They hang out at dive bars, love to shoot pool, and basically are not to be fucked with. Most have tattoos. The Plush Carpet is generally the more "feminine" of the two types. Plush Carpets dress to get laid,

A Metal Carpet

donning bright lipstick and sixties-style dresses or retro-preppy attire. Some even dress like flappers when going out on the town.

PHILOSOPHY
Metal—Bikini Kill is essential listening.
Plush—A smooth bikini line is essential grooming.

DISPOSITION
Metal—sullen.
Plush—femme fatale.

AVERSION
Metal—women with flattops, Kathie Lee Gifford.
Plush—sandals, barbecued ribs.

SEX
Metal—strap-ons.
Plush—only after putting clothes on a hanger.

REBUTTAL WHEN HIT ON BY A MAN
Metal—not applicable—men are too afraid to hit on Metal Carpets.
Plush—"Um, you have a penis."

A Plush Carpet

CK-1s

Sexually aggressive Hipster bisexuals are known as CK-1s.

ATTIRE/PRESENTATION
CK-1s always have young-looking faces and clean hair. Male and female CK-1s both prefer supershort cuts, although some males don a Prince Valiant look. Both look fairly androgynous, warranting responses from many like, "Damn, he'd be hot if he was a tassel," and, "I'd love to suck *her* dick."

PHILOSOPHY
No one is really straight.

DISPOSITION
Horny.

**LEADING COME-ON QUESTION WHEN ATTEMPTING
TO OUT SOMEONE**
CK-1 Males—Wanna wrestle?
CK-1 Females—Ever tried
GiGi crème wax?

AVERSION
Other CK-1s, herpes outbreaks.

SEX
CK-1s are notorious "outers" and rarely pay much attention to other CK-1s. They would much prefer a fling with someone who has never had a same-sex experience and flirt endlessly with their same-gender friends. One rarely encounters two CK-1s in a social clique because they are highly competitive. This competitiveness comes from their desire to have a sexual monopoly on their own turf. CK-1s tend to be on the airheaded side and say things like, "Fruit is good for you, right?"

A CK–1

DATING MAXWELLS, CK-1S, AND CARPETS

Common Turn-ons—*Penthouse Forum,* watching porn for a laugh, going to the mall for an ironic shopping spree, black leather footwear, tongue piercings

Major Turnoff—hippies

Maxwells, CK-1s, and Carpets tend to be noncommittal when it comes to dating. They are brimming with joie de vivre and don't like being tied down. Be sure not to mistake their forthrightness as a signal that they want to get liquid. Sexually defined Hipsters are big flirts, but they are just as selective as anyone else. Avoid taking Maxwells, CK-1s, and Carpets to gay-only clubs and bars. They prefer mixed company. Never take a Maxwell to a nude beach. Never take a Carpet to a dikey bar where the clientele look like drill sergeants. And never go to a swingers bar with a CK-1 for whom you've developed feelings. Maxwells, Carpets, and CK-1s often feel threatened if you develop friendships with other gays, lesbians, and bis, respectively, especially as things become more intimate.

Tattoos: They've Gone Suburban

In recent years, Hipsters have become belligerent about the tattoo craze that has taken over mainstream culture. Currently, it seems like everyone from Eminem to your typical Sigma Lambda Gamma pledge has one. Kids in the suburbs know that showing up at Friendly's on a Friday night with a badass tat will always impress their friends, and have begun raking yards for extra cash to pay for their tattoos.

Hipsters today must be more discriminating when selecting a tattoo for themselves. Here is an overview of various styles worn by non-Hipsters.

Bikers, Rednecks, and Neo-Nazis

Bikers, rednecks, and neo-Nazis tend to adorn their arms and shoulders with colorful tattoos. Many choose guns, knives, skulls, snakes, or their favorite motorcycle or car model. Others opt for phrases such as "American by Birth, Southern by the Grace of God." Hipsters avoid all of these styles, which tend to look better at White Pride rallies and rattlesnake shoots than on an art-school campus.

Gutter Punks

Gutter punks are never hip. They wear devils, Jesus images, pot leaves, or cartoon characters like Shaggy or Fat Albert smoking a blunt. Decorating one's body with a surplus of tattoos ensures perpetual unemployment. This prospect can be tantalizing to Hipsters, but most worry their parents will stop sending rent money if they fear it is being blown at tattoo parlors.

Sailors

Sailors get tattoos of women on their arms and shoulders. Immortalizing a favorite prostitute met on a port in the Philippines is a common choice for a sailor. Others decorate their shoulders with their battalion number or the emblem of their particular military branch. Eagles, flags, and anchors are similarly popular. Though most Hipsters should avoid these styles, Metal Carpets look especially deck with a kitschy sailor-style tattoo, provided they avoid beaver shots and disproportionately sized breasts.

Cock Rockers

Cock Rockers, like the members of Slipknot, Korn, Red Hot Chili Peppers, and their fans, follow "the more the better" rule. Cock Rockers prefer Native American imagery, headshots of dead rock stars like Janis Joplin or Kurt Cobain, flames, H.R. Giger–inspired pieces, and spirals around their breasts. These styles go well with mosh pits and at Floyd laser shows, neither of which are very popular with Hipsters.

Frat Boys and Sorority Girls

Frat boys and sorority girls get one tattoo that will be easy to hide from Mom, Dad, and potential employers. A dancing bear on the ankle or fraternity letters on the shoulder are popular choices for frat boys. Sorority girls choose a hidden heart, rainbow, or flower on their breast or pubic region to show their "naughty" side. Hipsters should sidestep all of these designs.

Homemade/Prison Tattoos

All types of homemade tattoos will make you look like you have been in prison, an image no Hipster wants to convey. Hipsters only go to jail overnight for protesting social injustices or for minor drug and alcohol infractions. Looking like you have a rap sheet when attending a Pipilotti Rist or Bill Viola opening can be a social setback.

Tattoos on the Face

Fin.

The Teardrop

Get real.

Selecting the Perfect Tat

A Tassel with a Deck Tat

As long as the face is not tattooed, Hipsters have free reign over their bodies when it comes to selecting a tat for themselves. Schmoozes, Polits, Loners, and other Hipster types who hope to interview for an office job should avoid tattooing the backs of their hands or their necks. Employers may think you are trying to steal from them.

Hipsters should choose a theme when deciding to sport multiple tattoos. Combining Celtic imagery with anime characters is midtown. They should also do research to find which tattoo artists do the best work. This is tricky, since asking Hipsters about their tattoos is taboo, but they can usually tell a good tattoo parlor from a bad one by watching the clientele it attracts. If a redneck or a biker is out front taking a piss, they may want to go elsewhere.

Picking a tattoo out of a book is never wise. Hipsters prefer to design their own. Otherwise, they run the risk of seeing Lenny Kravitz on a fin awards show with the same design. Tattooing sentences like "Want to see my tattoo?" or "Show me your titties" is always lame.

Pierce Wisely

Similar to tattoos, the piercing phenomenon has gone mainstream, causing many Hipsters to feel reticent about choosing a piercing for themselves. MTV has brought nose, lip, and eyebrow rings to the suburbs. Teens today pierce their faces at the mall while their mothers are picking out a towel set at Hecht's. In this piercing-friendly climate, those who don't know any better often mistake hilfigers with a surplus of piercings for Hipsters.

A fundamental rule is that having too many piercings is midtown. Overpiercing, wearing stretchers or plugs, or linking one piercing to another with a chain are styles reserved for Gutter Punks, Cock Rockers, Goths, and kids who were into Dungeons & Dragons in high school. Hipsters should also refrain from piercing their genitals, a ritual popular with sadomasochists, Wiccans, and fans of Anne Rice, none of whom are Hipsters.

Connecting Piercings with a Chain Is Fin

Hipsters who want to pierce their faces should decide upon a single location, such as the nose, eyebrow, lip, or cheek. Having more than one piercing on your face (ears not included) can make you look like an extra on the set of *The Crow, Part V.* Tongue piercings can be hip provided that one avoids waving their tongue around like Gene Simmons to allure strangers.

Metal as Fuck

Hipsters often use tattoos and piercings to add edge to their look. Similarly, many Hipsters listen to or play punk and metal to show how tough they are. Since Hipsters never get into fistfights, enlist in the military, or go hunting, they often use loud, guitar-driven music to burn off excess testosterone. Other Hipsters (especially WASHes, Bipsters, and Teeters) show nonconformist flair by being sarcastic or cynical or by making off-color remarks. Here are some things Hipsters may say or do to be punk or metal:

- Claim that The Beatles "suck shit" to be provocative.
- Nod approvingly when a buddy throws a recyclable can in with the regular garbage.
- Denounce vegetarianism as being pussy.
- Engage in hippie/Phish/jamband bashing.
- Adopt a pitbull.
- Discuss the art of Judas Priest while watching *Heavy Metal Parking Lot.*
- Make fun of electronic music and every band on Thrill Jockey.
- Order whiskey at a bar.
- Begin wearing black band T-shirts and wife beaters exclusively.
- Enter into a discussion about guitar pedals.
- Make a witty remark about having sex with one's mom, grandmother, or sister.
- Use the word "fucking as often as possible in phrases such as "Thursday fucking night."
- Call a diet-soda-drinking friend a "homo."

The WASH (Waitstaff and Service Hipster)

Definition: As the name implies, WASHes are Hipsters who work as bartenders, waiters/waitresses, in coffee shops, and sometimes at record and video stores. WASHes are noted for their idealism, but infamous for their cynical dispositions. They are the most common type of Hipster.

Question: Are you a Hipster?
Answer: Who the hell's asking? Hey, didn't you leave me a 10 percent tip the other night?

ATTIRE/PRESENTATION

WASHes understand the importance of a deck piercing and consider them crucial accessories. Where to pierce is up to the individual, but if you are a WASH you must have one or two. A WASH without a piercing is like a Jehovah's Witness without a bike. WASHes tend to think Salvation Army is an important design company in the same ranks as Gucci.

BACKGROUND AND UPBRINGING

WASHes have middle-class or lower-middle-class upbringings, usually attend public universities, and take great pride in the degrees to which they have cultured themselves, largely at their own expense. They are resentful of people who are born with a silver spoon in their mouth, and sometimes sneak a hair into their food. Similarly, WASHes who work at rental stores have been known to "mistakenly" let well-to-do customers leave with a copy of *Cocoon* instead of the movie they selected.

PHILOSOPHY
Working in an office is selling out.
You suck.

AVERSION
Fluorescent lights.

DISPOSITION
Crabby. Generally they are very nice people hiding behind hangovers, but sometimes they just suck.

THE HOME
WASHes have sarcastic senses of humor that often translate to a kitschy aesthetic in decorating. Many hang Loni Anderson posters on their walls or have a retro game like Hungry Hungry Hippo prominently displayed on a table. All have a magnet on their refrigerator with an image from a pulp paperback.

EDUCATION AND CAREER
WASHes choose "Undecided" as their major until their junior year in college, when they usually choose English or philosophy. In a similar way, WASHes make career decisions late in life. Many open restaurants or music stores of their own after talking about doing so for years. WASHes enjoy discussing how "the scene" has gotten lame well into their mid-forties, when they are usually tamed by the birth of their first child.

FORM OF TRAVEL
Ragged-out cars, bikes with baskets.

WARNING
There are five major things to keep in mind when interacting with WASHes, given their famously crabby dispositions:

1. When being waited on by a WASH, order quickly, never ask questions, and most important, tip well. To the WASH, karma is not a result of good versus evil, but tipping versus not tipping.
2. A WASH's happiness can be measured in direct proportion to whether or not they are required to wear a uniform. If you run into a WASH conforming to a dress code policy, beware.
3. Find out a WASH's schedule before calling. They take lots of naps and will not forgive those who wake them.
4. WASHes get defensive if you ask them what they do for a living or where they went to school.
5. Stand back should the WASH run out of cigarettes.

MODELS, ACTORS, AND ACTRESSES

Models, actors, and actresses who work in restaurants are sometimes mistaken for WASHes in urban centers such as Los Angeles and New York, but models and actors are generally not Hipsters. Striving to be on *All My Children* or in a Tampax commercial is never deck.

DATING A WASH

Common Turn-ons—tattoos and piercings, a love of fine cuisine, smoke rings, a complacent gaze, bikes with baskets, romantic walks at flea markets

Major Turnoff—briefcases

WASHes tend to date one another almost exclusively. They work high-stress jobs where they are routinely subjugated to high-maintenance and difficult customers. At the end of the evening, all the WASH wants to do is put back a few bronsons and blow off a little steam. Understandably, this combination of booze and moonlight often gives birth to romance. WASHes tend to seek out lovers who possess a little edge and, like themselves, are playfully cynical. Adopt a kitschy pop idol like Linda Ronstadt as your own and the irony-loving WASH will melt in your hands.

Waddup Bitch?! Hipsters and Their Greetings

Another key aspect of Hipster culture is knowing which type of greeting to use when saying hello. When answering the phone, Hipsters say "waddup," "hola," or "yo." Even a simple "hello" will suffice when expecting a more official call from parents or an employer. Answering the phone saying, "Michaelson residence, Todd is speaking" is ishtar. Schmoozes often say "*allô*" or "yellow." Loners have caller ID and rarely pick up the phone at all, unless a page is being returned by their dealer.

Similarly, Hipsters tend to choose fashionable ways of greeting one another in person. Here are some popular (and unpopular) greetings they use.

Devil Fingers
A greeting associated with metal and punk rock.

This type of greeting is generally a favorite of the Bipster, the Loner, and the WASH. The greeting has its origins in heavy metal culture, and Hipsters who employ Devil Fingers do so with a strong sense of irony. The greeting's rich "satanic" undertones are derived from followers of rock bands such as Rainbow and Dio, who were very fond of throwing out Devil Fingers during live shows.

To execute Devil Fingers, raise your arm in the air at a forty-five-degree angle, pointing your pinky and index fingers in the air while pressing the middle and ring finger against your palm with your thumb. For added effect, most Hipsters crinkle their face or show their front teeth.

Generally, the Hipster uses Devil Fingers late at night after a bit of revelry. When using it before sunset, the Hipster should avoid face crinkling and teeth displaying. Hipsters who use Devil Fingers generally have a passion for eighties metal that is paradoxically ironic and sincere.

Double Cheeking
Characterized by swift kisses from the side of one's mouth to a recipient's right and left cheeks.

Double Cheeking is a popular greeting for European Hipsters and Hipsters who consider themselves cultured and sophisticated. Most commonly, the UTF, the Schmooze, and the Polit are Double Cheekers.

If you are the initiator of this type of greeting, apply your pecks moving from left cheek to right while lightly bringing the body of the person being greeted close to your own. Never hug the recipient. Instead, put your hands lightly on his/her shoulders. Recipients will curve their faces inward to reciprocate your pecks with their own.

When greeting someone new, linger a bit, and move from cheek to cheek delicately (but don't be creepy). When greeting someone you are not fond of, Double Cheek very rapidly, barely making contact with the second cheek or avoiding contact altogether.

Keep in mind, if you Double Cheek someone once, you are obligated to do so every time you encounter this person again. Just like the old elementary school adage that you shouldn't chew gum unless you have enough to share, never forget to Double Cheek everyone in the group. Failing to do so is rude. It is also important that your mouth remains closed and you don't slobber. When kissing someone you don't like, or someone you feel is beneath you, make the sound "mmm-wa."

Single Cheeking
Characterized by a swift kiss to one cheek.

WASHes, Maxwells, CK-1s, and Carpets commonly employ this type of greeting. When initiating a Single Cheeking, always kiss the recipient's right cheek. Even left-handers should conform to this important rule, since kissing the wrong cheek will make you look like an amateur. Doing so is similar to eating your dinner with the salad fork.

The execution of a Single Cheek greeting is nearly identical to that of a Double Cheek greeting, but obviously only one cheek is kissed.

After applying your peck, pull back slightly with your hands still placed upon the recipient's shoulders and follow through with some kind words. The recipient need not kiss back, but he or she should maintain eye contact as the initiator pulls away to show approval. Single Cheeking tends to be less ostentatious than Double Cheeking and appeals to those who want to appear cultured, but not pretentious.

The Frontal
Greeting another with an embrace or hug.

This form of greeting is very popular with Clubbers, Neo-Crunches, and Hipsters who are big on brotherly and sisterly love. Other Hipsters should avoid this too-personal type of greeting with anyone other than very close friends. Most important, never use the Frontal to cop a feel. This is midtown.

If you are initiating this type of greeting, put your arms forward to acknowledge your intent. Never blindside or sneak your way into a Frontal or you will be stigmatized as a "grape" (greeting rapist) by your friends. Position your head to the left of the receiver's head as you place your arms around their body. Never put your hands or arms beneath the waist.

The Frontal can be very deck, especially when used by men to show their sensitive side. Like the Cheeking greetings, remember that after using the Frontal once, you will be committed to doing so for life.

The Frontal with Backslap
A hug accompanied by several firm pats on the back.

This type of greeting is used by fraternity types and men who are homophobic or concerned about looking gay. Hipsters generally avoid it.

The Full Frontal with Squeeze
A hug emphasized with a squeeze to the butt.

Though this type of greeting will generally warrant excommunication from the Hipster's circle of friends, the CK-1 is at times able to pull it off. No other Hipster type should even try the Frontal with Squeeze. Considered harmless flirts, CK-1s can usually execute this type of greeting and receive a laugh instead of a smack to the face.

The Lift
A form of greeting characterized by a slight but rapid elevation of the chin.

This form of greeting is most often practiced by WASHes and Bipsters when meeting new people. Though somewhat impersonal, the Lift is often used by Hipsters who are playing hard to get. Other Hipsters use the Lift in more vindictive ways, implying that the recipient should just keep moving. To increase the iciness of this greeting, apply the Lift with your arms crossed. This greeting can go awry if executed forcefully while wearing a hat.

The Tri-grip with Slide
A handshake consisting of four rhythmic movements.

A form of greeting almost always used by Teeters and sometimes by WASHes, Bipsters, and Neo-Crunches. This form of handshake consists of four rapidly executed movements. It begins with the standard shake, which is repositioned by rotating the hand upward and clasping the region between the thumb and forefinger, and then finally by sliding the hands palm-to-palm and folding the fingertips forward to be clasped by the similarly folded fingertips of the recipient.

Though many customize this greeting by creating specialized handshakes specific to their own group of friends, doing so is generally pretty fin. Complicated, multimovement handshakes often leave the recipient feeling confused or violated.

Step 1

Step 2

Step 3

Step 4

The Wall Street
The standard handshake commonly used by business types.

This type of handshake is too rigid and stodgy for most Hipsters, but is nonetheless used on occasion when mingling with non-Hipsters.

The Flava
A greeting associated with hip-hop culture.

This type of greeting is popular with Teeters as well as some UTFs and Clubbers. There are two variations of the Flava. The first variation is called the Full Flava. It's executed by crossing one's arms at the chest and then extending them outward, slightly higher than shoulder level. As the arms are extended, the middle and ring fingers should touch the palm of the hand with the other three fingers pointing outward.

Full Flava Step One　　　　　**Full Flava Step Two**

The second variation of the Flava is known as the Half Flava, and involves using only one of the movements described above (the choice is up to the individual). The UTF and the Clubber use the Full and the Half Flava in a tongue-in-cheek manner. Teeters, who are generally fans of *Yo! MTV Raps*, deliver this type of greeting without irony.

The Salute
A greeting generally used in the military denoting respect and discipline.

Only used by Hipsters sarcastically, after being asked to do something unpleasant.

The High Five
No explanation needed.

Popular with jocks. Hipsters aren't jocks.

The Pull Away
Characterized by extending one's hand and then pulling it away to run through one's hair.

This one is used only by morons.

The Snap and Gun
A snap of the fingers that is followed by pointing-gun hands.

See the **Pull Away.**

The "V" or Peace Sign
No explanation needed.

For jerrys only.

Choosing a Look

NASA Space Suit:

Is This Style

Deck or Fin?

Answer: This style is fin.

www.thehipsterhandbook.com and Other Deck Sites

www.alcoholreviews.com—Hip booze reviews by F. Sot Fitzgerald.

www.allmusic.com—A fairly comprehensive music research site.

www.brainwashed.com—Great electronic and indie reviews.

www.catch.com—The newspaper *and* the water cooler *and* the OxyContin.

www.craigslist.org—eBay for Hipsters.

www.doodie.com—Doodie.

www.dolphinsex.org—Dolphins!

www.emotioneric.com—Check it out; this dude's a trip.

www.fark.com—Funny Photoshop images and lots of Christopher Walken.

www.fatchicksinpartyhats.com—The name says it all.

www.fatmouse.tk—Fat mouse rules.

www.forcedexposure.com—Mecca for laptop geeks ordering records.

www.freewilliamsburg.com—New York's hippest neighborhood.

www.gopfun.com—Make fun of Republicans.

www.hoogerbrugge.com—Strange German Flash.

www.indymedia.org—Alternative media resource.

www.jambands.com—Just kidding.

www.nerve.com—Hipsters writing about sex.

www.makeoutclub.com—Hipster-only dating board.

www.members.aol.com/JesusImages—Funny as hell.

www.pitchforkmedia.com—Great music reviews.

www.rhizome.com—The new media art resource.

www.salon.com—The best on-line magazine for Hipsters.

www.slashdot.org—Tech and science news.

www.superbad.com—The strangest site on the Web.

www.theonion.com—The old standby.

Hipster Magazines

ArtForum—For all things art.

Black Book—For photographers and illustrators.

Bomb—Conversations with cutting-edge artists.

Bust—Keep abreast on all things feminist.

Contents—Two words: très chic.

Detour—Fashion, culture, and purty pictures.

Dutch—A fancy fashion mag.

Entertainment Weekly—Best read in private.

The Fader—A quarterly urban-lifestyle magazine.

Frieze—Keep up on contemporary artists.

Granta—An icon for new writing, even if it is a little crunchy at times.

Harper's—The quintessential Hipster magazine.

Index—Interviews with hip celebrities.

Maxim International—Deck.

McSweeney's—Dave Eggers' eclectic literary quarterly.

Nest—The beautifully designed magazine of interiors.

The New Yorker—For the sophisticated New Yorker.

Nylon—Trendy as fuck, but in a good way.

Paper—A great New York–based culture magazine.

Shout—An eclectic read that has featured writing by J. T. Leroy, Maggie Estep, and the Reverend Jen.

Smock—For artists or those who want to look like artists.

TimeOut—Hipsters love it, though none will admit it.

Vanity Fair—A fluffy magazine that tends to be less fluffy than other fluffy magazines.

Vegetarian Times—Learn how to marinate tofu.

Vice—Let us clarify: a dirty, fun, testosterone-charged vice.

Italian *Vogue*—Reading the American edition is like choosing yogurt over ice cream.

Wallpaper—Hipster decorating tip number one: have a copy of *Wallpaper* on your coffee table at all times.

While You Were Sleeping—Like *Vice*, but with fewer penis jokes.

Wire—Does anyone really read *Rolling Stone* or *Spin* anymore?

The Neo-Crunch

- - - - - - - - - - - - -

Definition: Post-Garcia hippies promoting idealism for a new century.

Question: Are you a Hipster?
Answer: That seems like a pretty superficial question, dude. Later—I have a serious falafel jones going on.

- - - - - - - - - -

ATTIRE/PRESENTATION

Neo-Crunches grow their hair long, stop bathing, and dress in dirty, tattered garments to disguise the fact that they are fairly comfortable financially. Female Neo-Crunches often cover their heads with decoratively bright bandannas or cowgirl hats, whereas Neo-Crunch males enjoy wearing a broken-in knit cap, even during the warmer months of the year. Some Neo-Crunches grow dreads, but it should be noted that white kids with dreads are fin. Many Neo-Crunches accessorize with an apple.

Excessive showering is avoided by the Neo-Crunch. They use the deodorant rock, which keeps them fresh for days (or so they claim). But remember, don't ever tell a Neo-Crunch he or she stinks. You will be given a well-researched lecture on how Europeans are wiser for not buying into the hypersanitary obsessions of the average American. "Deodorant is status quo, dude."

BACKGROUND AND UPBRINGING

Neo-Crunches have a somewhat homogenous upper-middle-class to upper-class upbringing. Growing up part of the leisure class often causes the Neo-Crunch to desire something deeper than the decadence and materialism of their parents. Neo-Crunches are not fully taken care of by their parents like the UTF, but do receive a little cush from the old man here and there. They claim not to need money, but readily accept it nonetheless.

PHILOSOPHY AND BELIEFS

Neo-Crunches are very idealistic. They are generally vegetarians or vegans and are passionate about human rights and the environment. Avoiding all things corporate is important to the Neo-Crunch, who has Big Brother phobias and worries that corporations are leaders in a larger worldwide conspiracy to control the individual (i.e., lock them up for smoking weed). Many have a great respect for dolphins and think we should be more like them.

AVERSION

Starbucks.

DISPOSITION

Heavy and light simultaneously, "like the Tao."

THE HOME

Neo-Crunches rarely put much thought into decorating their homes. They aren't interested in kitsch and generally decorate with furniture they find Dumpster diving. They are more concerned with filling their bathrooms and kitchens with environmentally friendly products like Ben & Jerry's ice cream and Tom's of Maine toothpaste. Some decorate with vitamin shelves or granola in recycled pasta-sauce jars. Many Neo-Crunches have hemp hammocks hanging in their backyards.

EDUCATION AND CAREER

Neo-Crunches are generally college-educated and obtain degrees from schools like Hampshire College, Antioch, and Evergreen State College. They are not picky about where they work, provided it is not a franchise. Your average Neo-Crunch is more concerned with finding work that won't require drug testing, dress clothes, or a haircut.

MODE OF TRAVEL
Bikes, Volkswagens.

HIPPIES VS. NEO-CRUNCHES
The Neo-Crunch is the latest incarnation of the outdated Hipster personality type, the hippie. Like their predecessors they are fond of saying "right on" and smoking pot. Neo-Crunches are prevalent on the West Coast, especially in Seattle and San Francisco, but can be found almost anywhere. Neo-Crunches are second in number only to WASHes. Since hippies and Neo-Crunches are often mistaken for one another, the chart on the next page offers some clues to help tell them apart.

DATING A NEO-CRUNCH

Common Turn-ons—marinating gluten, making bead necklaces, sharing a fatty, walking hand in hand with a "Free Tibet" sign, flannel sheets, bringing your own mug to a coffee shop

Major Turnoff—people who don't recycle

Neo-Crunches like to date people with optimistic outlooks. Cynicism is a drawback when courting the Neo-Crunch. "Beefy" breath is another big turnoff, so if you've had a burger, be sure to pop an Altoid before making your move. If you want to woo a Neo-Crunch, impress him/her with your knowledge of the Green Party, then discuss why Jerry Brown is a sellout. Nothing is more romantic to Neo-Crunches than swapping clothes so your partner can get subtle whiffs of your natural musk throughout the day. Neo-Crunches are always loyal and tend to want to settle down early in life. Use the term "grass roots" whenever possible and they will melt in your hands.

Hippies vs. Neo-Crunches

	HIPPIES	NEO-CRUNCHES
Political causes	GreenPeace, recycling, NORML	the antiglobalization movement, labor laws, NORML
Smoke weed out of	graphix bongs	glass pipes
Wear tie dyes	of course	never
Listen to	Grateful Dead, Phish, Widespread Panic	Wilco, Can, Black Star, Palace
End sentences by saying	"man"	"dude"
Refer to good marijuana as	kind bud, dank nugs, wacky tobacky	dope shit, trees, bubonic
Favorite magazines	*Relix, High Times*	*Utne Reader, Vegetarian Times*
Fragrance	patchouli and natural musk	natural musk only
Pass time by	playing Hacky Sack in a field	playing speed chess at a coffee shop
Musical instruments of choice	guitars, bongos, and tambourines	banjos and mandolins

A Day in the Life (*Slacker* Style)

Linda Locket is a WASH living in Wicker Park, Chicago, undoubtedly the most deck neighborhood in the city. She is twenty-five, recently graduated from the Chicago Art Institute, and bartends at a local bar called Hole in the Wall.

8:00 A.M.—Sleeping, of course.

9:30 A.M.—Wake up slightly when the sun begins to shine through my curtains. Turn on NPR and fall back to sleep listening to *Morning Edition.*

9:58 A.M.—OK, I'm up now.

10:00 A.M.—Wake up a friend with a call on my piece and agree to meet at the local coffee shop (not Starbucks) as soon as I get dressed.

10:03 A.M.—Put on my KFC name tag that I bought at the thrift shop the day before. It says Maggie.

10:07 A.M.—Carry my bike down the stairs, making sure the basket doesn't scrape against the wall.

10:18 A.M.—Grab a chair by the window at my favorite coffee shop and order a cappuccino with two shots of espresso, light on the foam, and with skim milk.

10:20 A.M.—Say hello to my friend Jill as she pulls up a chair beside me. Compliment her Dokken concert shirt (what a great find!) and then discuss boys, fashion, and how much we made in tips the night before.

11:11 A.M.—Tip the waitress 30 percent (good tip karma) and prepare to go home to work on my novel.

11:30 A.M.—Watch *The View*, my favorite dose of pop culture.

12:06 P.M.—Make a veggie burger. It's not deck to eat lunch this early, but I'm hungry.

12:38 P.M.—Put on a Dolly Parton record, inspiring music that helps me focus while I write.

3:00 P.M.—Pick up the phone. Mike wants me to sub out his shift. He's too hungover to work. I owe him a favor, so I agree. He'll relieve me at ten, leaving the remainder of the night open.

3:08 P.M.—Wash and shave my pits (underarm hair is jerry), but decide against doing my hair. It looks best a tad greasy.

4:09 P.M.—Arrive at Hole in the Wall late, but hey, it wasn't originally my shift anyway!

4:51 P.M.—Charge a frat boy six bucks for a Budweiser when he asks if our kitchen serves wings. What kind of a place does he think this is?

4:52 P.M.—Approach the juicer who just sat down at the bar. Cool tattoos! Celtic design is dope, though his sleeveless T-shirt is kinda Red Hot Chili Peppers. I bet he orders a pale ale. Red Hook, I'm thinking.

Kevin Stockwell is a Bipster who also lives in Wicker Park. He is a carpenter and is twenty-six years old.

4:52 P.M.—Think about what I want to order and decide upon a Red Hook. Damn, that bartender is hot! I wish I weren't too tired to polish.

4:53 P.M.—Take a sip from my beer and thank the cutie behind the bar.

4:54 P.M.—Check out her nancy as she puts my kale in the register.

4:55 P.M.—Put a two-dollar tip down. Tipping an extra buck will show her I'm interested.

4:56 P.M.—Smile when she says it's too quiet in here and gives me three bucks for the jukebox. I get a semi from the attention.

4:57 P.M.—Grumble under my breath when the frat boys at the corner table ask me to play R.E.M. I say I don't think they have any.

5:00 P.M.—Put on some Andrew W. K., Les Savy Fav, and throw in some Damn Yankees to be ironic. "Coming of Age" comes on first and I blush.

5:01 P.M.—Feel relief when she says "Nugent rocks," knowing she gets it.

5:05 P.M.—Wonder to myself if that cabinet I'm working on would look better without finishing. Exposed wood is deck.

Melissa Wui, a Schmooze originally from NYC, walks into the bar. She has lived in Chicago since '99 and graduated from the Chicago Art Institute last year with Linda.

5:10 P.M.—Enter Linda's bar. Damn, I was hoping Linda wasn't working. I wanted to invite her to the gallery opening tonight.

5:11 P.M.—Lean over the bar and give Linda a double cheek and say, "Waddup bitch." Say thanks when she compliments the Izod visor that I bought at Urban. I hope she doesn't ask where I got it. She doesn't.

5:12 P.M.—Sit down next to a Bipster at the bar. He's a juicer, but kinda rough around the edges.

5:13 P.M.—Tell Linda I was hoping she could come to the opening with me. Could be some important people there. Invite her to play Bingo next week instead.

5:14 P.M.—Light up Capri and order a vodka martini with extra olives.

5:15 P.M.—Ask what's up with the frat boys seated in the corner. We laugh and catch up on the latest gossip on the scene.

5:17 P.M.—Pull my piece from out of my Gucci bag. It's my friend Todd; he says to hurry over to the opening. Arto Lindsey may be there. Finish my drink and tell Linda that I have to run.

5:18 P.M.—Tell Linda I'll swing by late when she invites me to a warehouse party tonight and say adieu. Linda gives me Devil Fingers as I leave. She is so deck.

5:19 P.M.—Eye the boy at the bar and nod in approval, making sure his back is turned. Linda rolls her eyes and smiles. Linda doesn't know how fine she is, I think to myself.

5:20 P.M.—Mount my Vespa and remember I forgot to pick up my new business cards. I can't believe they messed up and used Courier font on the last ones. Do I look like a Java programmer?

Meanwhile Kevin sees an opportunity to strike up conversation with Linda.

5:20 P.M.—Tell the bartender I didn't mean to eavesdrop, but the party tonight should be deck. I tell her I know the promoter. She says she's definitely gonna check it out. I tell her my name is Kevin. She says she will be there. Her name is Linda.

5:21 P.M.—Think to myself that I hate the name Linda. I dated a spoiled UTF with that name. She lied and told her parents I went to Brown. Cunt.

5:28 P.M.—Realize my pit bull has probably pissed on the floor by now and turn down a drink offered by Linda. I should go home and walk him.

5:29 P.M.—Thank Linda for the bronson and tell her I'll get her on the party list tonight, plus one.

5:30 P.M.—Put on my mirrored shades as I leave in case she missed them on the way in.

Andrew Finch, a Polit originally from Richmond, Virginia, enters the bar. He was an English major at VCU and moved to Wicker Park last month to get closure on a relationship gone sour. Linda is one of his few acquaintances in Chicago.

7:33 P.M.—Pull my leather-bound journal with the "Meat is Murder" sticker out of my bag. Place it on the bar next to my e. e. cummings anthology and my Drum cigarettes. Line them up side by side.

7:34 P.M.—Say hello to my friend Linda and give her a single cheek.

7:35 P.M.—Ask Linda what's up with the frat boys in the corner playing quarters and yelling. She rolls her eyes.

7:36 P.M.—Worry that the frat boys are looking at me. Did they hear me making fun of them? I don't want to get my ass beat. They probably think I'm gay since I'm sporting mod duds.

7:37 P.M.—Order a Maker's Mark and start writing. Linda asks what I am working on and tell her some experimental poetry. It is about Carrie. She tells me to get over her. I tell her about the poetry slam at the coffee shop next week and invite her to come.

7:44 P.M.—Wonder if Linda hates me. She seemed noncommittal when I invited her to my poetry reading.

8:03 P.M.—Feeling blocked with my writing. I can't find a good rhyme for "rodomontade."

8:40 P.M.—Order a beer and realize I may be too shellacked to write. Plus, I am missing Carrie. I can't believe she fell for that cheesy guy. He works out and smells like English Leather cologne.

9:20 P.M.—Think to myself, Pencils are deck. Maybe I should start writing in pencil.

9:59 P.M.—Notice the bar has gotten really loud. Linda asks me to go to a party with her. Probably feels sorry for me. I feel pathetic. I wonder if Fitzgerald felt this way when Zelda went crazy.

Linda is kicking herself for taking this shift. Tips are awful and those frat boys stiffed her altogether. At least it's almost time to leave.

9:59 P.M.—Tell Andrew I am getting off in a sec and ask him if he wants to come to the party with me. He agrees.

10:19 P.M.—Wonder where the fuck Mike is. He was supposed to be here at ten.

10:23 P.M.—See Mike finally carrying his ass in the door. He looks stoned. I pack up my things.

11:06 P.M.—Arrive at the party and it is packed. The juicer I met earlier got me on the guest list! I feel a tad nervous knowing he is here.

11:07 P.M.—Walk around and check out the scene. I introduce Andrew to some friends and can tell they think his mod suit is a little much. They are always such bitches with new people.

11:18 P.M.—Spot the juicer from the bar across the room and give him the eye. He approaches and I thank him for getting us in.

11:29 P.M.—Think to myself, What's with all these garage bands who sound like the Strokes?, when some band I've never seen before starts playing. Poseurs.

11:29 P.M.—Grab a drink at the absinthe bar and feel duped. It tastes like straight vodka.

11:32 P.M.—Double cheek Melissa, who just walked in. She says that Arto was a no-show at the opening. Kevin walks over again and introduces himself to Melissa. She gives me a thumbs-up when he isn't looking and grabs my ass.

11:37 P.M.—See my Neo-Crunch friend Anne and ask her where her new cronkite is. She says she dumped him. She got turned off when he starting whipping out an air guitar at the Hives show. Plus, she is vegan and always hated how he would kiss her after eating burgers.

11:38 P.M.—Laugh with Kevin, who spots two carpets making out in the corner. He asks me if I've ever kissed a girl. I say no. I don't want to seem midtown, so I tell him I've always wanted to though. This polishes.

11:51 P.M.—Notice that Andrew and Melissa are hitting it off.

11:54 P.M.—Talk casually to Kevin, who out of the blue whips out a power line—"Wanna go back to my place to smoke up?" I accept.

Later at Kevin's place.

12:14 A.M.—Sit down on Kevin's sofa and he puts on some Sade. I think to myself, Do I look like a chipper??? Sade is such predictable seduction music. I feel panicked until I realize he's being funny.

12:15 A.M.—Tell him he'll have a better chance wooing me with Pat Benatar. He thinks I'm joking. I'm not; Pat Benatar rules.

12:17 A.M.—Excuse myself to his bathroom—it's clean. No pubes on the seat or anything.

12:20 AM—Try to pee but I'm almost too nervous. Finally I have success.

12:21 A.M.—Check Kevin's medicine cabinet for Prozac or Paxil. I don't need any more psychos in my life.

12:22 A.M.—Notice he uses Prell. What's up with that?

12:23 A.M.—Walk back into the living room and Kevin is playing the Johnny Cash gospel album. He just may get some after all!

12:25 A.M.—Smile and say thanks when Kevin serves me a gin gimlet with a bendy straw. Deck. We smoke a joint.

12:28 A.M.—Move in for a kiss and some steamy lip action begins. I take the sunglasses hanging from the neck of his T-shirt and put them on the coffee table. I realize it has been three months since I last got liquid.

12:28 A.M.—Grab his Highway 66 belt buckle and he stops my hand. Why do deck guys always hold out?

Kevin

12:28 A.M.—Think to myself, she's hot, but it's deck to hold out. Anyway, I jerked off earlier to *Girls Gone Wild*.

Linda

1:02 A.M.—Think about calling Melissa to see if she is with Andrew. Keep kissing Kevin instead.

1:51 A.M.—Cuddle and make out while watching a *Magnum P.I.* repeat. Think to myself, It was a good day, as I fall asleep.

A Girl Gone Wild

The Teeter

Definition: Young-at-heart Hipsters who are most commonly associated with skateboards, graffiti, and tagging.

Question: Are you a Hipster?
Answer: Huh? You need a bag or something?

ATTIRE/PRESENTATION

Teeters have youthful appearances. They are especially fond of hooded sweatshirts and Vans sneakers. Baggy pants and wallet chains are also popular. Unlike other cell-phone-carrying Hipsters, Teeters accessorize with pagers. This prevents them from being held accountable for missed appointments. "I missed your page" is usually code for "Don't call when I'm practicing my ollie."

BACKGROUND AND UPBRINGING

Teeters have their origins on the streets of L.A., Atlanta, Chicago, and New York, where life in an urban jungle forces many to find inventive ways to pass their time and express themselves. Teeters believe life is meant to be enjoyed, not intellectualized, and often think Bramante, da Vinci, and Michelangelo are pasta sauces. This Hipster personality type has spread far and wide; Teeters can now be found in cities, suburbs, and the country alike.

PHILOSOPHY AND BELIEFS
Lots of deep and profound shit.

AVERSION
Sirens.

DISPOSITION
Stoned. Teeters are usually high and never pass up a good wake-and-bake. Rolling blunts from Dutch Masters cigars is the method of choice, but Teeters aren't too choosy. They always cough when inhaling their herb. This gets them more stoned and saves them money, which is important, since they are generally poor. Teeters address one another as "son," "dog," "bitch," and "nigga." There is never any irony in their delivery.

THE HOME
Teeters live at home with their parents or crash on their friends' sofas. When Teeters wear out their welcome on the couch, just tell them a detective or an ex stopped by looking for them while they were gone. This is the easiest way to get rid of them without having to hear a biting rebuttal of "Dude."

EDUCATION AND CAREER
Teeters have high school educations, but rarely go to college. They would much rather perfect their half-cab pivots or tag subway cars than sit in a classroom all day. "That shit is wack, nigga." Similar to UTFs, Teeters don't have jobs. Nevertheless, some Teeters have been known to sell nickel bags to make a buck. Many say they are "pushing boundaries" by not working, but we aren't sure what this means.

MODE OF TRAVEL
Skateboards, subway.

WARNING
Teeters are notorious moochers. They show up empty-handed at parties and make their way immediately to the fridge to grab the last cold bronson. Strangely, people tolerate this type of behavior from them. Teeters flatter with lines like, "Your shit looks dope" to smooth over any infraction.

Though Teeters are generally poor and soft-spoken, they tend to attract beautiful and wealthy partners in love. People who date them are always extremely hot and tend to worship the ground they walk on. Teeters often depend financially on those they date and commonly borrow money, but rarely pay it back.

ALPHA TEETERS

Teeters usually travel and operate in large packs. They generally have one leader, commonly referred to as the **Alpha Teeter.** The Alpha Teeter might suggest that everyone go grab some nachos, and the pack would be sure to follow. Teeters treat their Alphas with respect and would never let them roll or light their own blunts.

SNOWBOARDERS AND SURFERS

Snowboarders and surfers (who share cultural similarities with Teeters) are not Hipsters. They are usually too unfashionable and culturally unaware to qualify. Besides, anyone who uses the term "shredding" is generally pretty fin.

DATING A TEETER

Common Turn-ons—food in the fridge, cable TV, long walks on the beach with a blunt, kung-fu movies, people who don't "hassle" them, being able to smoke weed in your crib, getting laid

Major Turnoff—sushi restaurants

Teeters don't want to invest much energy in dating. They are content to keep things casual and prefer just having sex without all the formalities and complications of a relationship. If you have a place of your own to take the Teeter, half of the conquest has already been won. Teeters regularly sleep on their friends' couches or live at home with their parents, so having a place of your own can be very alluring to them. In fact, many Teeters will stick around just to have a place to crash. If you have food in your fridge, the Teeter's eyes fill with *amore!* Let the Teeter male fall asleep after sex and he will never leave you. Let the female Teeter do a mural on your bedroom wall and you will be partners for life.

Indigenous Zones of the Hipster in the United States and Canada

New Orleans—Lower Garden District
Brooklyn—Williamsburg
Manhattan—Lower East Side
Montreal—The Plateau
Toronto—College and Clinton
Chicago—Wicker Park
Seattle—Belltown
Richmond—The Fan
Philadelphia—Olde City
Vancouver—Commercial Drive
Austin, Texas—Clarksville
Minneapolis—Whittier
Los Angeles—Silverlake

Washington, D.C.—The U District
Boston—Davis Square
Miami Beach—Lincoln Road
San Francisco—Inner Mission
Detroit—Hamtramck
Baltimore—Mt. Vernon, Fells Point
Atlanta—Little Five Points and Cabbagetown
Milwaukee—Riverwest
Knoxville, Tennessee—Fort Sanders
Cleveland—Coventry

The Ivy Leagues for Hipsters

Hipsters understand the importance of a good education and generally strive to obtain BAs from private universities. They occasionally attend public and state schools, but often feel out of stride in Greek environments. Hipsters never pledge sororities or fraternities and uniformly avoid colleges known for their keggers. Receiving a BS is not unheard of, but most Hipsters receive degrees in the liberal and fine arts. Schools that attract Hipsters usually have strong art programs and at least one professor named Paula. Colleges such as Oberlin and NYU have large Hipster populations, whereas Berkeley is stuck in a sixties mentality and is totally jerry. Here are some popular choices for Hipsters looking for the perfect education.

New York University, Manhattan, New York
Hipness Grade: A-

Throw a copy of Final Cut Pro and you'll hit a film student on this Hipster-heavy campus. Throw a hash pipe and watch them wrestle one another to grab it first. NYU Hipsters are often from New York and make the move from the Upper East Side to downtown to have the experience of roughing it during their tenure as students.

University of Iowa, Iowa City, Iowa
Hipness Grade: C

Their creative writing department was the first in the country, and noted UI graduates include Flannery O'Connor, John Irving, Robert Bly, Tracy Kidder, Philip Levine, and Raymond Carver. Needless to say, this college is a favorite for Polits. You could say that Iowa is a ripe breeding ground for literature and corn, but UI students prefer that you don't. On the downside, the abundance of jocks in football jerseys substantially lowers their grade.

RISD (Rhode Island School of Design), Providence, Rhode Island
Hipness Grade: A-

Nestled in the college town of Providence, RISD is one of the hippest colleges in the Northeast. The typical RISD student believes that trying hard is passé and embraces an absurdist worldview to cope with heavy workloads. They all love a good Brown joke, but hey, who doesn't? RISD alumni often form artist groups with geeky names like Forcefield to stay in touch after graduating.

CalArts, Los Angeles, California
Hipness Grade: B-

CalArts is a very posh school about thirty minutes north of Hollywood. It's popular with Hipsters who are animators, painters, and performance artists. Students tend to be a little cocky, but reminding them that Walt Disney founded CalArts will settle them down.

Vassar, Poughkeepsie, New York
Hipness Grade: B

This college specializes in the avant-garde and attracts theater aficionados. Hipsters here like to get naked and paint their faces white while quoting esoteric poetry in unison onstage.

California College of Arts & Crafts, California
Hipness Grade: B

This schizophrenic school has two campuses—an architecture and design school in San Francisco and a fine arts department in Oakland. The glassblowers here are usually white Rastafarians, the painters accessorize with splatters, and the film and video students dress in black and rarely see the light of day. Both campuses tend to have a Hipster playing a saw for spare change.

Brown, Providence, Rhode Island
Hipness Grade: B-

Brown's modern culture and media department attracts Hipsters of all backgrounds, but each one graduates knowing how to use the word "exegesis" in a sentence. Stop by Ocean's Coffee Shop during the school year to eavesdrop on some great PC conversation.

Oberlin College, Oberlin, Ohio
Hipness Grade: A

This small college in Ohio has a student body that is 94.6 percent Hipster (provided you exclude the conservatory). The English, religion, and creative writing departments are equally strong, attracting Hipsters in droves. Students enjoy lively dancing on campus at the 'Sco, which is strangely reminiscent of a high school dance filled with catty conversation and no-smoking signs. After graduating, relocating to Manhattan to pursue a career in the arts or with a nonprofit is an unwritten requirement.

Bennington College, Bennington, Vermont
Hipness Grade: B-

Bennington has strong visual arts, painting, and dance departments and a "coed campus," which in actuality constitutes one
male for every ten females. Many get the small-town blues after
being here too long and liven things up by dyeing their hair several
different shades of blue, self-mutilating, or tattooing flames on their
arms. These practices prompted one local to say, "Oh, you don't
wanna go to Bennington—they do weird things up there on the
hill—real weird things."

Virginia Commonwealth University, Richmond, Virginia
Hipness Grade: C+

Hipsters and non-Hipsters peacefully coexist at VCU, since the frat
culture found at most larger schools is nearly nonexistent. Their
strong mass communications and photography schools are especially popular with Hipsters. Grace Street is the place to be seen
after hours, provided you have a tattoo and a piercing. Watching
the Medieval Club stage battles beneath the statue of Robert E. Lee
is a perk you won't find in their college catalog.

Wesleyan, Middletown, Connecticut
Hipness Grade: C+

Don't fuck with the political activists at this small liberal arts school
in Connecticut. Their president's office got firebombed not too long
ago by a disgruntled student. Most have lightened up and prefer
juggling and other forms of passive resistance, especially during
Zonker Harris Day, a festival named for the pot-smoking Doones-
bury character. Hipsters who go here should always clarify which
Wesleyan they attend, since there are like five hundred of them.

Cornish College of the Arts, Seattle, Washington
Hipness Grade: B-

Flannel and tousled hair are the norm on this super-crunchy campus. Their motto is "You will not be neglected or ignored as an
anonymous art student, nor will you be constrained by arbitrary
time factors. We believe in you." Doesn't that make you feel good?

Earlham College, Richmond, Indiana
Hipness Grade: B-

Some Hipsters go to this tiny Quaker liberal arts school hoping classes will be held in silence. They aren't. Hipsters tend to receive a strong education at Earlham because there is nothing else to do but study in Richmond, Indiana.

University of Chicago, Chicago, Illinois
Hipness Grade: C+

University of Chicago has always been a favorite of Polits. Bertrand Russell was a visiting professor in the late 1930s, and Saul Bellow received his graduate degree here. Plus, gargoyles are deck and can be found on most of the earlier buildings. The school was founded by John D. Rockefeller, which can be troubling to some capitalist-loathing Polits.

Evergreen State College, Olympia, Washington
Hipness Grade: A+

Evergreen State College is the kind of school where you earn high marks just for being a Hipster. Calvin Johnson is an alumnus of Evergreen. He is also the founder of K Records, whose slogan is "Exploding the teenage underground into passionate revolt against the corporate ogre since 1982." Bruce Pavitt, who founded SubPop records and coined the term "grunge," also went to Evergreen. Willy G. Stotson went here too, but he hasn't done anything notable.

Barnard College, New York, New York
Hipness Grade: B-

Barnard College is considered one of the strongest liberal arts schools on the East Coast, attracting countless Hipsters to their all-women campus. Many Carpets enjoy the outstanding English department and, of course, the booty.

Other Colleges Where Hipsters Can Be Found

American University—Washington, D.C.
Atlanta College of Art—Atlanta, Georgia
Bard—Annandale-on-Hudson, New York
Colorado College—Colorado Springs, Colorado
Dartmouth College—just kidding
Emerson College—Boston, Massachusetts
Hampshire College—Amherst, Massachusetts
Maine College of Art—Portland, Maine
Memphis College of Art—Memphis, Tennessee
The Milwaukee Institute of Art and Design—Milwaukee, Wisconsin
Minneapolis College of Art and Design—Minneapolis, Minnesota
Parsons School of Design—New York, New York
Pratt Institute—Brooklyn, New York
Reed College—Portland, Oregon
Sarah Lawrence—Bronxville, New York
Skidmore College—Saratoga Springs, New York
Swarthmore—Swarthmore, Pennsylvania
UNC Wilmington—Wilmington, North Carolina
University of Texas—Austin, Texas

The Polit

Definition: Extremely literary Hipsters who have philosophical approaches to politics and existence, but are romantic in matters of love. The term Polit (pronounced **pah**-lit) is an amalgamation of the words "political" and "literary."

Question: Are you a Hipster?
Answer: Shut up, fascist.

ATTIRE/PRESENTATION

Many Polits have thick-looking skin and a mole or two on their neck and face. They accessorize with berets, newsboy hats, eighties band buttons, and wire-rimmed glasses. Polits carry notebooks in their leather shoulder bags containing bits of poetry they have written and words from philosophers and writers they find useful. Polits also carry a copy of one of the following: *The Stranger* by Albert Camus, *The Communist Manifesto* by Karl Marx, *The Fountainhead* by Ayn Rand, Che's biography, or an anthology by Sylvia Plath, e. e. cummings, or Rilke.

BACKGROUND AND UPBRINGING

Polits have middle-class upbringings and usually come from the suburbs. Some are accused of having oedipal issues with their parents. They resent the insinuations, but dig the literary allusion.

PHILOSOPHY AND BELIEFS

Marxism is deck. Unlike Neo-Crunches, who are political in a naïve and lighthearted way, Polits are realists with more cerebral world-views. The Polit would much rather debate Kierkegaard than search for ways to achieve world peace. Polits generally define themselves as existentialists and say things like, "The decisions I make are who I am." This can frustrate waiters attempting to get them to decide between a Reuben and a chef salad. Polits are often critical of tech-nology. Most prefer writing letters in longhand to sending e-mail, and consider television to be an opiate of the masses."

AVERSION

John Grisham, Republicans.

DISPOSITION

Melancholy. Despite their cynical exterior, Polits are the most romantic of the Hipster personality types and are always loyal to the ones they love. Though Polits usually prefer coffee and other stimulants, they often take to booze and begin carrying flasks when agonizing over a relationship gone sour. A tad melodramatic, maybe, but flasks are undeniably deck.

THE HOME

The expatriate lifestyle of Hemingway and Gertrude Stein is the Polit ideal, and they spend most of their time away from home writing and smoking hand-rolled cigarettes in coffee shops. More introverted Polits have writing rooms at home and have been known to decorate them with mounted deer heads and gun racks to add edge to their work.

EDUCATION AND CAREER

Frequently, Polits have degrees in English and/or literature and are proud of being able to debate the works of William Faulkner, Flannery O'Connor, and Martin Amis. Many also create their own majors, such as Biblical References in Western Writing. They generally work jobs affiliated with universities, become freelance writers, work in publish-ing, or organize events for nonprofit groups. Polits who are editors often get fired for writing bold notes in the margins like, "This para-graph sucks" or, "You sound a little bit like a Nazi in this passage, don'tcha think?"

MODE OF TRAVEL

Vespa or bike. Some drive cars, but feel guilty about supporting the oil industry.

THE POLIT POET

Many Polits are poets. Here are some of our favorite first lines from Polits we know:

- "Crashing through the jaded pillars of your skull, we unite lickety split"
- "Juniper, Juniper, your love tooketh me to Jupiter"
- "I defoliate world orders in fresh factories of frost, sha la bing"
- "How will it
               be
     in   side of you I
  have never seen, like strawberry cobbler fairs"
- "Stop teaching the babies to kill filthy astronaut"

DATING A POLIT

Common Turn-ons—well-edited love letters, going to lectures, Che T-shirts, paper cuts, hand-rolled cigarettes

Major Turnoff—laughter

Nothing could be sexier to the Polit than sitting at a bar with the right tassel or cronkite, discussing the merits of socialism and Marxism with Billy Bragg playing in the background. Polits are easy prey, since they are constantly on the lookout for that special someone. When dating a Polit, write long letters and poems that reference the works of Melville and Eliot. Make sure you proofread them before you lick that stamp; most Polits correct misspellings and grammatical errors as they read. Commitment is a turn-on; Polits are prone to lengthy tirades about the merits of monogamy. Don't be afraid to cry. Polits generally express love for the first time during a good weep session. Though most Polits enjoy cerebral mates, others have been known to sacrifice debating Kierkegaard for a handsome face.

Working for the Man

As we've learned, Hipsters come in all nationalities, ages, and socioeconomic brackets. Nonetheless, there is an undeniable hierarchy within Hipsterdom based primarily upon career and education. Ideally, the Hipster is able to avoid work altogether. Unemployment provides Hipsters with plenty of time to create art and hang out in coffee shops debating politics with friends. UTFs and unemployed Hipsters are generally at the top of the hierarchy, since they have the most time to refine their cool.

Similar to Eskimos, who have several words for "snow," Hipsters have many terms for receiving a check from the parents. The most commonly used phrase is "getting the cush," but "picking the berries," "waxing oedipal," "parimony," "daddimony," and "changing the diaper" have equivalent meanings.

Since unemployment isn't realistic for most, UTFs sometimes get lonely during the day. They may develop an addiction to *The Bold and the Beautiful* or begin drinking at noon. UTFs who don't have other UTFs to spend time with sometimes resort to taking part-time jobs to ward off this loneliness.

In this section, we have outlined professions that are popular with unfortunate Hipsters who have to work.

Bringing Home the Kale: Popular Hipster Professions

- **Architect**—Many Hipsters graduate with degrees in architecture and enjoy the merging of right- and left-brain activity required by the field. Architecture allows them to be creative and logical at once. Hipsters who have apprenticeships with established architects can remain hip, but once architects secure jobs on their own, a metamorphosis often occurs and they become Yuppies.
- **Art Handler/Gallery Worker**—Art handlers and gallery workers enjoy spending the day surrounded by cutting-edge art. Work of this nature can be an excellent stepping-stone for the artist's

career. Many Hipsters claim that handling priceless work inspires them through osmosis. More resourceful Hipsters sneak their own art pieces into the show and gush over their work to unsuspecting attendees. On the downside, Hipsters in this industry often feel like serfs when they aren't invited to the important parties sponsored by the gallery for which they work.

An Art Handler

- **Bike Courier**—Drinking Mountain Dew, bungee jumping, and saying you are into extreme sports is fin. Hipsters who like a rush of adrenaline become bike couriers instead. This job frees them from office work, and the thrill of weaving in and out of traffic can be quite a rush. Plus, they can always take the day off by saying their bike is in the shop. Note: Hipster bike couriers are usually stoned and should wear helmets.

- **Book Dealer**—Book dealers are generally aspiring writers who spend countless hours unloading shipments of books and perusing publishing catalogs to decide what titles to stock. They often write their own fanzines, have deck box cutters adorned with rock band stickers, and claim to prefer working in a bookstore to selling out to a publisher. Mention *The Divine Secrets of the Ya-Ya Sisterhood* in their presence and they will be sure to reveal one "divine" secret—Oprah Book Club shit like that sucks ass.

- **Carpentry/Furniture Restoration**—Bipsters who enjoy working with their hands often become carpenters. Some find pleasure designing ornate furniture, while others prefer building inexpensive utilitarian fare. Still others restore antique furniture bought at flea markets, which they sell to yuppies who are willing to shell out three hundred berries for a coffee table. None are fond of the phrase "Jesus was a carpenter."

- **Chef**—A passion for food drives many Hipsters to become chefs. They pay close attention to what vegetables are in season and often use ingredients from their own gardens exclusively. Some become culinary spiritualists who help to discern which food types are best suited for their clients based upon astrological signs, complexions, or digestive histories. Hipster chefs enjoy cooking garlicky meals for friends to pass along the stench they are notorious for having themselves.

- **Dog Walker**—A popular profession for Hipsters whose parents pay their rent but don't give them any spending money for the weekend. Dog-walking Hipsters earn a few extra berries to support the other costs of living, like drinking and buying gas for the moped. Accidentally losing a dog while scrambling to answer a cell phone is a common blunder for Hipsters carrying too many leashes. Careers in dog walking are a mainstay for UTFs and Neo-Crunches.

- **Editor**—Non-Hipster editors simply enjoy the nuances of language and like to spend time ensuring that grammar is used correctly. Hipsters who are editors are often writers inside a Trojan horse waiting to blindside the publishing world with the mind-blowing manuscripts that they will someday get around to writing. Be careful to edit even the most trivial of correspondences when communicating with an editor. He or she considers the improper use of language bourgeois.

- **Fashion Designer**—This is a popular profession, given the Hipster's hyperawareness of fashion. Hipsters who are fashion designers are notorious for being catty. They gossip, often critiquing the style (or lack thereof) of friends and acquaintances at parties. Fashion designers are always working; every social engagement becomes a research project about what people are wearing. Their wildly imaginative visions can turn a coffee stain on a tie into a national trend that will appear on the runways the following season.

- **Freelance Writer**—Hipsters who say they are freelance writers do so just to have a response when you ask them what they do for a living. Nobody actually makes a living doing this.

- **Full-Time Student**—Many Hipsters feel displaced after obtaining an undergraduate degree. In more severe cases, removal from an academic environment causes vertigo and prolonged headaches for the Hipster. Many return to school because they simply can't function as civilians. More commonly, Hipsters return to academia because they have an aversion to working and are looking for an excuse to quit. Most are merely delaying the inevitable. UTFs, on the other hand, just have nothing better to do.

- **Grip or Gaffer**—Grip and gaffer work is very common for film students and Bipsters trying to schmooze while they work on their own film projects on the side. They tend to wear all black and love a good penis joke.

- **Illustrators**—Hipster illustrators aren't qualified to do anything else for a living. They missed out on obtaining an education because they were scribbling in a notebook instead of taking notes. Plus, many refused to read textbooks that weren't printed in a font they found pleasing. Some, like the illustrator of this book, prefer the title "drawer."

- **I've Got a Van**—You've doubtless seen the posters plastered on telephone poles: "Man with a Van." Call the number on the flyer and you'll sometimes find a Hipster on the other end. Buying a van to help others move and transport valuables is a great way to make some quick money and avoid working in an office. Just don't drive around elementary schools too frequently. A man with a van who drives in close proximity to children will end up in a police lineup.

- **Kinko's**—Be very afraid of Hipsters who work at Kinko's. Hipsters don't "go postal"; they "go Kinko."

- **Massage Therapist**—Massage therapists are generally hippies who work in shops that also sell crystals and New Age music. Hipster massage therapists, on the other hand, never have a shop of their own and tend to perform house calls exclusively. They advertise by word of mouth, and give thirty-second teasers at parties hoping to lure new customers into giving them a call. Therapists who moan with pleasure when giving someone a massage have short careers.

- **Movie Store Clerk**—Hipsters who work for movie rental stores tend to be somewhat antisocial, but don't be put off if they respond to your questions with a grunt. Many spend so much time watching movies that their vocal cords atrophy from lack of use. Though most are very accommodating and helpful, others get their angst out by playing gore-heavy movies like Peter Jackson's *Bad Taste* on the in-store monitors.

- **Musician**—For many Hipsters, getting signed to a label is a dream come true. Unfortunately, signing with a major label is selling out, and signing with an indie label won't pay the bills. It's a no-win situation. Most musicians supplement their income by temping or working a service job. Others resign themselves to eating only Ramen noodles. Some take jobs as lounge players at the Holiday Inn, a very deck thing to do for those who savor irony.

- **Performance Artist/Theater Actor**—Theater actors decide early on that soap operas, commercials, and Hollywood fare are beneath them. They learn acting techniques such as the Strasberg, the Adler, and the Meisner methods, and sacrifice a big paycheck for the sake of higher art. Performance artists enjoy doing jazz hands while covered in chocolate syrup. Actors who have other actor friends exclusively suffer from stunted maturity and often have the emotional dispositions of small children.

Musicians Who Do
Rock Jumps
Impress the Tassels

- **Production Assistant**—Production assistants are generally Hipsters fresh out of art school who want to get involved with film or television. When working for larger companies like CBS, the PA is given ample freedom and becomes integral to the creative process. When working for individuals and smaller companies, the PA is essentially a secretary with an art-school background or an Ivy League degree. Jotting down phone numbers of power players from the boss's Rolodex while he/she is at lunch is a noteworthy job perk. Most PAs find the workday goes by quicker if they concoct elaborate fantasies about killing their bosses.

- **Projectionist**—Art-school types with degrees in film often work part-time at the local independent film house as projectionists. Sneaking someone into the projection room for a quickie is a common practice, but Hipsters should be careful not to bump into the projector or forget to change the reel. Hipsters who stay in this profession too long are in danger of becoming social rejects who walk the streets mumbling movie lines to themselves.

- **Record Store Clerk**—Immortalized in Nick Hornby's *High Fidelity*, the record-store Hipster is often quite smug, but hey, not all record store clerks are music snobs. Many are actually very accommodating and helpful. Just don't ask if they have *John Tesh Live at Red Rocks* or other cheesy fare and you will be surprised at how friendly many can be.

- **Sidewalk Salesperson**—Gutter punks and hippies are generally associated with this type of career, but one will occasionally encounter a Neo-Crunch setting up shop on a busy street corner. Most Hipsters avoid this degrading work, but Hipsters who are out of work sometimes have to make a buck however they can. Though most forms of street vending are pretty fin, Hipsters can make some quick kale by selling their own artwork or clothing they designed. Neo-Crunches should be advised to wear a hat if serving food. Licking a stringy hair found in one's Sno-Kone is bad for business.

- **Stripper**—Hipsters call it burlesque. And they are dancers, not strippers.

- **Subway and/or Street Performer**—Hipsters who have grown weary of working nine-to-five jobs in fields unrelated to their artistic expertise drop out and become street performers. They are promised a large audience when performing in a big city and don't have to sacrifice their vision by conforming to someone else's standards. The more savvy performer will try to appear homeless to get sympathy dollars from the crowd. Mimes, performers who bang on garbage cans, and break-dancers who do backspins on crowded subway trains are generally too annoying to be considered hip.

- **Temp Worker**—Temp work is unpredictable. For some, it is mindlessly dull drudgery that requires one to stare at the wall and wait to be excused for lunch by a skanky, middle-aged lady with ashtray breath. For others, it can be very demanding work where one is yelled at by angry tyrants for forgetting that someone important is on hold on that phone with nine hundred buttons. In the best cases, the Hipster has time to write, catch up on reading, send out résumés, or do some design work while sitting at his/her desk. In the worst cases, the Hipster gets an ulcer and loses the will to live. Regardless, the true joy of temping is stealing office supplies. Most Hipsters temp at one time or another, but burn out quickly on the cubes and the fluorescent lights. Others are let go for failing to understand that you don't really dress down on "dress-down Friday." Wearing a Metallica shirt to work doesn't jive with the image Morgan Stanley is trying to project.

- **Video Editor (Final Cut Pro and AVID)**—Film and video editing are very popular professions for Hipsters. Loners especially like Final Cut Pro because they can edit video on their home computers. Traditionalists who edit using the AVID don't like to be sneaked up on, since they are generally very focused. Don't touch their equipment unless you want to experience their wrath. Editors who use wipes, dissolves, and motion effects to create psychedelic homemade music videos are generally pretty fin.

- **Waiter/Waitress/Bartender/Counterperson**—Service work is by far the most common profession for a Hipster. If you are prone to complaining the waitstaff always has too much attitude, chances are you've never worked in a restaurant yourself. The money can be okay, but this type of work sucks.

- **Web Designer and Web Developer**—Before the Internet crash, Hipsters infiltrated the dot-com world in swarms. Working for an Internet company suited the Hipster lifestyle to a T. Hipsters could dress casually and come and go as they pleased, and the environment was rarely autocratic or stifling. CEOs pretended to be Hipsters themselves, and for once in history it was cool to work a straight job. Best of all, Hipsters were given the opportunity to play video games all day. Today, Hipsters who still work for Internet companies have become discouraged by downsizing. Being laid off can be humbling, but losing a hard drive filled with downloaded MP3s is a tragedy.

Choosing a Look

The Laptopper:

Is This Style Deck or Fin?

Answer: This style is deck.

The Job Interview

There are times when even the Hipster has to go on the dreaded office job interview. When doing so we recommend several things. First of all, dress up. The casual dress interview died with the dot-com era. Today, most employers will immediately dismiss you as a serious candidate if you show up in a T-shirt and jeans. Being on time, well-groomed and well rested, and deleting intramural sports from your résumé are recommended for everyone. In addition, Hipsters should keep the following in mind, given their proclivity for the unconventional:

- Study the sports section, in case a sports fan interviews you.
- Don't tell the interviewer you are hungover if you stumble over your words.
- Don't call the person interviewing you "dude."
- Cover your tattoos and remove lip, eyebrow, and nose piercings.
- Do not print your résumé on colored paper to be artsy.
- Don't wear Pumas with your suit.

We're Looking for a Straight Shooter

- Don't ask if any hot chicks work in the office.
- Don't ask if they test for drugs.
- Avoid using the word "fuck" and other strong expletives.
- Don't ask if you can come in at eleven, should they decide to hire you.
- Don't introduce yourself with the Devil Fingers greeting.
- Remove the band buttons from your shoulder bag, especially if they say things like "Revolting Cocks" or "Dr. Octagonecologyst."
- Leave immediately if they say they are looking for a "straight shooter." You won't be happy there.

Note: If a Hipster is interviewing you, ignore this list.

Choosing a Look

The Cowboy:

Is This Style Deck or Fin?

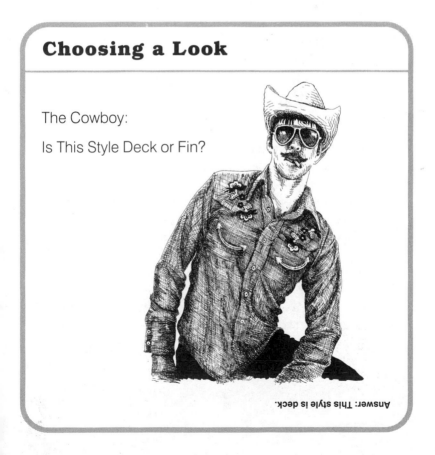

Answer: This style is deck.

The Bipster

Definition: Blue-collar Hipsters who shun art-school pretension and have little patience with leisure-class Hipsters. The term Bipster is derived from combining "blue-collar" with "Hipster."

Question: Are you a Hipster?

Answer: Do I look like some spoiled rich kid? Fuck that.

ATTIRE/PRESENTATION

Bipsters care little about fashion and wear only three colors: black, blue, and white. Both genders have arms filled with tattoos and a soft place in their heart for denim. Facial hair (especially goatees) is a big plus for Bipster males, while females often wear white T-shirts without bras. The Bipster woman enjoys teasing the eye with her bralessness and then looking sullen and pissed at the foolish male who tries to sneak a peek. Both genders accessorize with pit bulls.

BACKGROUND AND UPBRINGING

Bipsters are usually from middle-class to lower-middle-class backgrounds. They are a very common breed of Hipster and often grow up in the South or the Midwest. Most Bipsters are too interested in books and art to get involved with sports in high school, but enjoy a good arm-wrestling match during lunch.

PHILOSOPHY

Do it yourself. Bipsters don't like to hire others to do jobs they can learn themselves. Many are secretly huge fans of Martha Stewart. Bipsters are staunch realists and avid readers, but tend to prefer nonfiction titles like *Zen and the Art of Archery* and *The Autobiography of Johnny Cash.* Most consider gyms to be unnatural and get their exercise at work or by doing rock kicks at home while listening to metal.

AVERSION

Belle and Sebastian, and bands that use vocoders.

DISPOSITION

Confident. Bipsters have great pride in their abilities, but most have a vulnerable side. Some get a little misty watching *MacGyver.*

THE HOME

Any true Bipster has at one time or another built a loft bed out of discarded plywood. To the Bipster, IKEA is "pussy." One should be wary of splinters when visiting a Bipster's home. Most Bipsters enjoy putting art prints on their walls with staple guns.

EDUCATION AND CAREER

Bipsters usually graduate from public colleges or trade schools, if they attend college at all. The Bipster is no less mentally capable than any other personality type; they just by nature shun the "spoiled" art-school lifestyle. Many Bipsters are carpenters, painters, bike couriers, or do construction. Others work in bike shops, tattoo parlors, and on movie sets as grips, gaffers, and set builders. Bipsters are always pro-union, and some believe Woody Guthrie may have been an incarnation of the Buddha.

MODE OF TRAVEL

Motorcycles and bikes are popular with the Bipster, who wouldn't be caught dead on a Vespa.

TESTOSTERONE IRONY

Since being homophobic is never hip, Bipsters have fine-tuned the art of testosterone irony. The true Bipster knows how to use terms such as "fag" and "pussy" in very fashionable ways. A Bipster might say, "I can't hire him to work in the bike shop with me, he'd play fag rock all day," or "That rhinestone shirt Mike wears is pussy." Bipsters are fond of using terms that reinforce their own masculinity, but know to use such terms only as adjectives. A Bipster, for instance, would not say, "I'm going to get some pussy tonight." That would be midtown.

BIPSTERS AND REDNECKS

Like the Loner who has definite dweeb tendencies, the Bipster has to be careful not to act like a redneck. This is generally not a problem for Bipsters who build movie sets or work side by side with stoners from bike shops, but when working with rednecks who whistle at women and accessorize with grease stains, there is always the danger that the redneck's Budweiser-driven lifestyle will rub off. The chart on the next page explains some key differences between rednecks and Bipsters.

DATING A BIPSTER

Common Turn-ons—Being cool with the fact he/she was arrested that one time last summer, tattoos, working the grill, dog lovers, duct tape

Major Turnoff—vegans

Male and female Bipsters seek mates who are, respectively, very feminine or masculine. They never seek out prudes or meatheads but delight in a partner who is somewhat traditional when it comes to gender roles in dating. Male Bipsters would never cut their date's food at a restaurant, but to them holding a door is common courtesy. Female Bipsters won't settle for a wimpy Loner in a Belle and Sebastian shirt. They like a man with dirty hands who doesn't have to call AAA to fix a flat. Some Bipsters (especially those who work on movie sets or behind a camera) enjoy videotaping sex. And it is the rare Bipster who doesn't enjoy a good spanking in the bedroom. Don't sleep in too long—they like to rise early and enjoy the day. When becoming more serious with a Bipster, put some money in the bank in case he/she goes on strike. To find bliss with the Bipster, daydream together about restoring an old home in which you'll raise a family.

Bipsters vs. Rednecks

	BIPSTER	REDNECK
Are experts at making	Lofts	Moonshine
Wear T-shirts with	British flags	Rebel flags
Pay dues to	Unions	NRA
Outdoor festival of choice	Ozzfest	Indianapolis 500
Slick back hair with	Natural oil	10W-30
Slick back hair for extra hold with	Dippity-Do	10W-40
Tend to have	Classism issues	Racism issues
Beers of choice	Guinness, microbrews	Coors Lite, Busch
Music	Andrew W.K., Gram Parsons, Motorhead, Hank Williams, Sr.	Travis Tritt, Bob Seger, Hank Williams, Jr.
Favorite meat	Steak, ribs	Rabbit, squirrel
Outdoor Hobbies	Camping and mountain biking	Hunting and rooting
Call gay men	Indie rockers	Fags
Artistic expression	Painting abstract works on large canvases	Painting "swamp dog" or "Bocephus" on large trucks

HIPSTERS AND THE ARTS

Hipster Music:
I Want My MTV Disconnected

Hipsters take great pride in their music collections and are very particular about what they choose to listen to. Music helps define the personal identities of Hipsters, breaking them down into subcategories such as emo Hipsters, rockers, and laptop Hipsters.

Hipsters add the words "neo," "post," or "neo-post" to current genres to demonstrate their superior knowledge of music and its place in history. Music must be important and/or ironic, and not being open to a myriad of different types of music is fin. With the exceptions of contemporary Christian, jazz fusion, world, cock rock (rap metal by bands such as Slipknot) and New Age music, Hipsters listen to everything.

Since Hipsters never settle for the predictable, we have skipped some of the more obvious titles and bands (*Revolver, Pet Sounds,* The Ramones, *Odelay,* Velvet Underground) in favor of underappreciated works. Here are some records every Hipster should own, categorized by decade.

The Groovy Sixties

1. Johnny Cash—*At Folsom Prison* (1968)
Johnny Cash (or "the Man in Black") is the quintessential badass, and this is his finest hour. He did time for smuggling amphetamines in his

guitar case and smashed the Grand Ole Opry's lights for turning its back on him when he was down. Totally punk rock.

2. **The Who—*The Who Sell Out*** (1967) The Who rocked in the early days, and *The Who Sell Out* features some great faux ad jingles that were a funny critique on commercialism. Roger Daltry was always a frado, but no one smashes a guitar like Pete Townshend.

3. **The Kinks—*The Kinks Kontroversy*** (1966) The reissue contains the hit single "Dedicated Follower of Fashion," which is one of the hippest Brit-pop songs ever written. Frontman Ray Davies has inspired the work of a multitude of Hipsters and is one of the most consistent songwriters of our time.

4. **Serge Gainsbourg—*Comic Strip*** (1966–1969) OK, so this is actually a posthumous collection featuring Serge's work between '66 and '69, but it's a good one. Gainsbourg was never a wally, but somehow managed to get hotty Brigitte Bardot into the sack, a testament of his music's power to allure. Refer to this French performer as "Serge" to show you are in the know, and dismiss his incestuous relationship with his daughter as him "being French."

5. **Stan Getz/João Gilberto—*Getz/Gilberto*** (1964) Wanna have a margarita, sit in the sun, or spend the afternoon getting liquid? Getz and Gilberto will make it happen. Metal Hipsters claim to hate loungey Brazilian jazz, but they are fags. This record features Astrud Gilberto, whose voice is as soothing as a summer breeze.

6. **Elvis Presley—*From Elvis in Memphis*** (1969) Many things considered great actually suck. One example is Iggy Pop. Elvis's '68 comeback special is another. Fortunately, flushed with the ratings success of the TV show, Elvis recorded a soul/country/rock/gospel album with power and sensitivity, tapping the intensity of the Memphis Horns, the twin tragedies of his mother's death and his troubled marriage, and all the painkillers his

doctor could prescribe. It remains one of his final triumphs before he got really fat.

7. Nick Drake—*Five Leaves Left* (1969) That Volkswagen commercial that used "Pink Moon" was fin. Regardless, Nick Drake was cute, superhip, and British, which was a big plus in the

Choosing a Look

The Jackie-O:

Is This Style Deck or Fin?

Answer: This style is deck.

sixties. He was making "shoegazing" music before it was even a genre. Plus he died before he could start sucking. .

8. **Rolling Stones—*Aftermath*** (1966) Mick Jagger in his prime. Need we say more?

9. **The Byrds—*Sweetheart of the Rodeo*** (1968) Gram Parsons created alt-country and said a big "fuck you" to the music industry by turning the folky sounds of the Byrds into something totally new. Steel guitars are very hip.

10. **Captain Beefheart and the Magic Band—*Trout Mask Replica*** (1969) Produced by Frank Zappa and containing the line, "A squid eating dough in a polyethylene bag is fast and bulbous, got me?" *Trout Mask Replica* is essential listening.

The Sexy Seventies

Note: The seventies were too deck to limit our list to ten selections.

1. **The Residents—*Eskimo*** (1979) True Hipsters, the Residents preferred remaining incognito. This explains the large eyeball masks, top hats, and tuxedoes they always wore in public and on this record's cover. Who else has done a record in homage to Eskimos?

2. **Slade—*Slayed?*** (1972) This British band paved the way for Quiet Riot and was among the first to misspell words in titles like "Cum on Feel the Noize," a very deck thing to do.

3. **Joy Division—*Unknown Pleasures*** (1979) Joy Division helped introduce keyboards to punk rock with this debut, risking an ass-beating

from the technology-hating traditionalists who controlled the genre at the time. Every male Hipster over the age of thirty has an *Unknown Pleasures* T-shirt.

4. **Funkadelic—*Maggot Brain*** (1971) George Clinton made looking like a pimp from outer space cool. Get on the mothership with *Maggot Brain*, the strongest Funkadelic/Parliament release.

5. **Syd Barrett—*The Madcap Laughs*** (1970) Syd put the hallucinogenics in Floyd's tea, sung about "cold steel rails" and his bike, started a musical sensation, and then went insane. Deck.

6. **Lynyrd Skynyrd—*Second Helping*** (1974) Yes, we are being serious.

7. **Roxy Music—*Country Life*** (1974) Bryan Ferry and Brian Eno combined art rock and glam rock with unparalleled success. They also drained all the juice from both spellings of their names; nobody hip named Bryan or Brian has been born in over two decades.

8. **Black Sabbath—*Master of Reality*** (1971) Before *The Osbournes*, there was Black Sabbath. Before Black Sabbath there was the Prince of Darkness; he just didn't have a band.

9. **David Bowie—*Hunky Dory*** (1971) Bowie is the main inspiration for the Glam Rocker and the CK-1 personality types, as well as a Hipster icon. Now if he would just retire, we'd feel more confident about his Hipster status remaining intact.

10. **The Clash—*London Calling*** (1979) Our incredibly hip friend Kevin had this to say about this record: "I used to have this guy living below me who wore those silly, sleeveless English-flag T-shirts. He played the Clash constantly, which I could hear through the tissue paper that we called a floor. I also heard him having loud sex with two girls at the same time once. The Clash rule."

11. **Patti Smith—*Horses*** (1975) Just kidding—no one really listens to this record, although everyone pretends that they do.

12. **The Slits—*Cut*** (1979) The first riot-grrrrls, the Slits showed that attitude was more important than musicianship. Mick Jones had to tune their guitars for them, but no one ever had to show them how to rock.

13. **Cheap Trick—*Heaven Tonight*** (1978) Come on, you know you like it.

14. **Can—*Tago Mago*** (1971) We had to pick a Kraut rock band and it was a toss-up between Can, and Neu!, and Kraftwerk. Can won because they have the deckest name.

15. **Curtis Mayfield—*Superfly*** (1972) The title says it all.

16. **Blondie—*Parallel Lines*** (1978) In the seventies, Debbie Harry was every schoolboy's wet dream and every schoolgirl's idol. *Parallel Lines* is a pop classic.

The Fresh Eighties

1. **Beastie Boys—*Paul's Boutique*** (1989) This is the *White Album* for the post-Boomer Hipster. Here's our favorite line: "I'm adamant about living large with the white sassoons and the looks that kill makin' love in the back of my Coupe De Ville."

2. **Motörhead—*Ace of Spades*** (1980) Cool T-shirts, cool sideburns, nasty-ass mole. *Ace of Spades* is a favorite of most Bipsters.

3. **Public Enemy—*It Takes A Nation of Millions to Hold Us Back*** (1988) It took a nation of millions to get that big-ass clock around Flav's neck, but they don't come any decker than P.E. Where else can you find Fred Sanford and David Bowie sampled in the same tune?

4. Tom Waits—*Rain Dogs* (1985) Even though he sings like Cookie Monster, Tom Waits is one of the greatest songwriters of all time, and this is his masterpiece.

5. Prince—*Sign 'o' the Times* (1987) Before he changed his name to that pretentious sign thing, Prince kicked ass. This double album rocks even though shortening of "of" to "o'" is almost as dorky as using the term "o'er."

6. Sonic Youth—*Daydream Nation* (1988) Sonic Youth was the royal family of the indie movement in the eighties. This was their last great record before signing with a major label. Sonic Youth have blood on their hands, though, since they introduced Kurt Cobain to Geffen.

7. The Pogues—*Rum Sodomy & the Lash* (1985) Non-Hipsters have Jimmy Buffett. Hipsters have Shane MacGowan. This is irreverent bar music for those with taste.

8. Devo—*Freedom of Choice* (1980) Nerdy geeks who made doing nerdy geeky things like wearing flower pots as hats not so nerdy or geeky.

9. N.W.A.—*Straight Outta Compton* (1989) Dr. Dre, Ice Cube, MC Ren, and the always-underrated Eazy E introduced the world to gangsta rap with this release. It was priceless to watch suburban kids sing along to lines like "Straight outta Compton is a brotha that'll smother yo' mother and make ya sister think I love her."

10. Gang of Four—*Solid Gold* (1981) The title was ironic for a band who spent most of their lyrical time taking shots at capitalism. The Red Hot Chili Peppers may be their bastard child, but we can forgive them.

The Indie Nineties

1. **Pavement—*Slanted and Enchanted*** (1992) Two preppy, post-post-punk art-school nerds and a urine-stained hippie trip over heaven on their way to the Scrabble board. Steve Malkmus was the indie world's Marky Mark and had all the girls swooning. Thankfully, *he* never did underwear ads.

2. **Air—*Moon Safari*** (1998) Who knew elevator music could be so deck? Apparently every Hipster on the planet. Categorized as French disco, Air made cheese accessible to even the most hardened rockers.

3. **Stereolab—*Emperor Tomato Ketchup*** (1996) No, they didn't rip off Kraut rock predecessors Neu! They merely perfected their sound. Retro-futurism is hot! In the future will there be future-retroism?

4. **A Tribe Called Quest—*The Low End Theory*** (1991) Q-Tip needs to stop hanging out with frados like Leonardo di Caprio and P. Diddy if he wants to gain our respect back, but *Low End Theory* was the party album of 1991 and still sounds fresh today (in an early-nineties kind of way).

5. **PJ Harvey—*Rid of Me*** (1993) PJ Harvey is an amazingly talented artist who with time will be spoken of in the same breath as Bob Dylan and Tom

Waits. Plus she looked really hot in Hal Hartley's *The Book of Life*.

6. **My Bloody Valentine—*Loveless*** (1991) Hipsters who enjoy saying "ethereal" or get chills hearing flangers always choose this as their top pick from the nineties.

7. **The Orb—*Adventures Beyond the Ultraworld*** (1990) Though Squarepusher or Aphex Twin could just as easily be on this list, The Orb has more crossover appeal among Hipsters. *Ultraworld* helped define the ambient house movement. In other words, it is a cool disc to get stoned to.

8. **Kool Keith—*Dr. Octagonecologyst*** (1996) Porn, murder, rape, gynecology, and the phattest beats of the nineties, *Dr. Octagonecologyst* was as cutting-edge as it was tasteless. Pop in the instrumental version when entertaining the easily offended.

9. **Fugazi—*Repeater*** (1990) These aren't the kind of guys you want to spend very much time with (they all have sticks up their asses in a very D.C.-PC kind of way) but they definitely know how to rock. Their music is strong enough to not be overshadowed by their crammed-down-your-throat anticapitalist politics.

10. **Tie: Guided by Voices—*Bee Thousand*** (1994) and **Yo La Tengo—*I Can Hear the Heart Beating as One*** (1997) If you are a Hipster woman who falls for nerdy types, you probably love these records. If you are a guy and own them, then absolutely anyone on the planet can kick your ass. Regardless, they are both genius and undeniably part of the Hipster canon.

Newer Artists Kicking Some Ass This Decade

White Stripes
Yeah Yeah Yeahs
Le Tigre
Gorillaz
Hot Snakes
Múm
The Shins
Clinic
The Fucking Champs
Cannibal Ox
Dismemberment Plan
Fennesz
Notwist
Prefuse 73
Zero 7
Interpol
Marumari
Ladytron
The Streets
Sahara Hotnights
The Mooney Suzuki
Anti-Pop Consortium
Dead Meadow
Black Dice
Trabant

Acid Mothers Temple & The
   Melting Paraiso U.F.O.
Lightning Bolt
Gillian Welch
Ryan Adams
High on Fire
The Hives
Kid606
Les Savy Fav
RJD2
Mr. Lif
Cave-In
Liars
El-p
The Boggs
Circulatory System
Vladislav Delay (a.k.a. Luomo)
The Microphones
Queens of the Stone Age
Regenerated Headpiece
Mastodon
The New Pornographers
Loose Fur
Out Hud
The Rapture

Hipster Literature: If You Haven't Read These Works, at Least Pretend You Have

All Hipsters are selective about what they read and wouldn't be caught dead reading garbage written by Tom Clancy, Belva Plain, or Nora Roberts. Hipsters often allow hip books to dangle

from their bags to show others how cutting-edge they are. All Hipsters should read Jack Kerouac. And if you've never read Fyodor Dostoyevsky's *Crime and Punishment*, run to your closest book dealer right now. Here are some additional titles all Hipsters should read.

1. **Dennis Cooper—*Frisk***

   So cool that JT Leroy wants to be him. All of Dennis Cooper's books are already Hipster classics.

2. **J. D. Salinger—*Franny and Zooey***

   Salinger was an unbelievably deck Hipster who got so tired of the publishing world he decided to go into hiding. *The Catcher in the Rye* had too many hippie undertones to qualify, making *Franny and Zooey* his most essential work for Hipsters.

3. **Nick Hornby—*High Fidelity***

   Fuck the movie. The book was better.

4. **Jacqueline Susann—*Valley of the Dolls***

   Want to look deck reading in a park or on the subway? Pick up this kitschy classic. *Valley of the Dolls* has more sex and deceit than an episode of *Dynasty*.

5. **Terry Southern—*Red-Dirt Marijuana and Other Tastes***

   This collection of hilarious, drug-inspired short stories shows why this Hipster icon was deck enough to appear on the *Sgt. Pepper's Lonely Hearts Club Band* cover.

6. **Haruki Murakami—*The Wind-up Bird Chronicle***

   This may be another story about vanishing ladies, but it's his best story about vanishing ladies. Murakami is a genius.

7. **David Foster Wallace—*Infinite Jest: A Novel***

   Actually, scratch this one. It's too damn long. Hipsters just hear that it's good. If they actually read it they'd see that Wallace is a poseur.

8. Ben Marcus—*Notable American Women: A Novel*

This one has a deck cover and will look very hip in your hands at a coffee shop while sipping an espresso. Oh yeah, it's a pretty good read too.

9. Dave Eggers—*A Heartbreaking Work of Staggering Genius*

An essential read that will enable you to make fun of how pretentious Dave Eggers is.

10. Jim Thompson—*The Killer Inside Me*

Jim Thompson is Stephen King's favorite crime writer, but Hipsters don't care about that. He was writing darker work in the 1940s than Mr. King could ever dream up. Thompson was even employed to write two screenplays for Stanley Kubrick, *The Killing* and *Paths of Glory*.

Poets Hipsters Adore

William Blake
Jorge Luis Borges
Lee Ann Brown
The Brownings
Charles Bukowski
William S. Burroughs
Anne Carson
e. e. cummings
Eazy-E
Maggie Estep
Allen Ginsberg
John Keats
Beth Lisick

Pablo Neruda
Sharon Olds
Sylvia Plath
Edgar Allan Poe
Ezra Pound
Rainer Maria Rilke
Percy Shelley
Bucky Sinister
Patricia Smith
Gertrude Stein
Tom Waits
Kevin Young

11. Anaïs Nin—*Delta of Venus*

Bisexual erotica that's as sexy as it is literate. Hipsters know that masturbation can be educational.

12. Thomas Pynchon—*Mason & Dixon*

Throw out your American History 101 textbooks; Pynchon's reimagining is much more hip. Hipsters like the Caffeine Theory, which suggests that drinking coffee and smoking can create a more frank and honest world. Conspiracy theorists who try to decipher hidden meanings about masons and the number 23 are pretty fin.

13. Raymond Carver—*Cathedral*

His protagonists are always plebeians, and Hipsters enjoy saying "plebeian." Plus his stories are usually one cigarette in length.

14. Paul Auster—*The New York Trilogy*

Paul Auster is a stylish, page-turning author whose existential writing rivals the work of Camus. *The New York Trilogy* is a perfect read, and hopefully Auster will never pull that prequel shit like George Lucas and ruin a good thing. His recent allegorical novels about kids who can levitate and talking dogs have been crap.

15. Ernest Hemingway—*A Moveable Feast*

Page after page of cafés, fine wine, sex, and F. Scott Fitzgerald bashing. Hemingway's *A Moveable Feast* encapsulates the Paris expatriate experience better than any other novel of its kind.

16. Hunter S. Thompson—*Hell's Angels: A Strange and Terrible Saga*

Thompson joined the Hell's Angels to write this inside account about the notorious biker gang. He got his ass beat, but a great book came out of the experience. We long for the hallucinogenic gonzo reporting found in his later writing, but this is nonetheless his most cohesive work.

17. Don DeLillo—*Great Jones Street*

About a rock star who is sick of being a commodity. Deck.

18. Raymond Chandler—*Farewell, My Lovely*

No one made the streets of L.A. seem cooler than Chandler's smart-ass protagonist Philip Marlowe. We dig the Coen Brothers' take on Marlowe in *The Big Lebowski*, where he is turned into "the Dude."

19. Eugene Zamiatin—*We*

Better than *Brave New World* and *1984*, and ripped off by both.

20. Albert Camus—*The Stranger*

This classic existentialist work is hanging out of the backpack of every Polit in the country.

21. Martin Amis—*London Fields*

Filled with pop culture, sex, and laughter. Saying you haven't read *London Fields* is like showing up at MOMA without a shirt.

22. Iceberg Slim—*Mama Black Widow*

A story about a black queen written by an ex-pimp. Deck.

23. Henry Miller—*Tropic of Cancer*

This book was banned until 1961 and branded obscene by the Citizens for Decent Literature, two very distinct honors for Hipsters.

24. Zadie Smith—*White Teeth: A Novel*

A hilarious debut impressively written when Zadie was only twenty-four years old. Some Hipsters are moved by her graceful prose. Others will just enjoy staring at her sexy author picture.

25. David Sedaris—*Naked*

Funny as hell and perfect for self-deprecating Loners who feel awkward in their own bodies.

26. Carolyn Keene—*Nancy Drew's The Secret of the Old Clock*

Nancy Drew rules.

Choosing a Look

The Animal Accessorizer:

Is This Style Deck or Fin?

Answer: This style is fin.

131

Hipster Cinema:
Rolling Out the Red Carpet,
or The Oscars Suck Ass

Hipsters are film aficionados who take pride in their disdain of Hollywood fare that stars Meg Ryan, Julia Roberts, Tom Hanks, and Robin Williams. When it comes to trite cinema, these actors are the Four Horsemen of the Apocalypse, although others such as Mel Gibson, Denzel Washington, Sandra Bullock, Vin Diesel, and Whoopi Goldberg are quickly gaining ground. Weeding through the crap at the video store can be tough for Hipsters, given the abundance of titles like *Mr. Deeds* and *Men in Black II,* but we want to help. Here are a wide selection of titles that comprise the Hipster canon of essential film.

1. ***Buffalo '66*** d. Vincent Gallo (1998) Vincent Gallo may be an egomaniac, but this film is as touching as it is funny, and you'll be pulling out those Yes albums you swore you'd never touch again after hearing the soundtrack. Christina Ricci looks hot in her preanorexic girth, and Gallo looks cute too, in a Jesus-in-tight-pants kind of way.

2. ***Suspiria*** d. Dario Argento (1977) Italian horror master Dario Argento's classic work is as visually lush as it is scary. We like his next flick, *Inferno,* too, but

had to disqualify it since Keith Emerson of ELP did the sound-track.

3. *Manhattan* d. Woody Allen (1979) Some prefer *Annie Hall*, but Diane Keaton's unfortunate wardrobe in that film pushes *Manhattan* to the forefront for most Hipsters.

4. *Down by Law* d. Jim Jarmusch (1986) Jim Jarmusch and Tom Waits team up to make a Hipster classic. *Stranger than Paradise* is good too, but Waits is simply more deck than *Paradise* star and ex–Sonic Youth guitarist Richard Edson.

5. *The Seventh Seal* d. Ingmar Bergman (1957) Known as the grandaddy of the "art film," *The Seventh Seal* depicts a chess game with the Grim Reaper. Deck.

6. *The Killing* d. Stanley Kubrick (1956) We were going to include *Reservoir Dogs*, but then we realized that Kubrick had already made that movie with *The Killing*.

7. *Blazing Saddles* d. Mel Brooks (1974) Brooks is so talented, he can turn a fart joke into highbrow comedy. The racial jokes are dated in an *All in the Family* kind of way, but who can resist a black man in a Klan suit saying, "Where all the white women at?"

8. *Duel* d. Steven Spielberg (1971) Spielberg's often-forgotten ticket into the mainstream. *Duel* is a white-knuckler from the time when he was indie.

9. *Crumb* d. Terry Zwigoff (1994) This documentary on cartoonist Robert Crumb is as disturbing as it is funny. We discover that the "Keep on Truckin'" cartoonist is a misogynist who jerks off to his own comics. If you think that's frightening, wait until you meet his family.

10. *Orphée (Orpheus)* d. Jean Cocteau (1949) In this surreal French classic, Death is chauffeured in a Rolls and escorted by a posse on motorcycles. Cocteau created the motorcycle-thug archetype. The descent into the underworld is much cooler than the one imagined in *Hellraiser 2*.

11. *Drugstore Cowboy* d. Gus Van Sant (1989) Hard to believe people once thought Matt Dillon was cool, but he *is* in this movie by indie favorite Gus Van Sant. Best of all, Robin Williams and Matt Damon are nowhere to be found. Beat wisdom provided by William S. Burroughs adds just the right Hipster flair.

12. *Brazil* d. Terry Gilliam (1985) A film so visually stunning, many forget that it's damn funny too. Film-geek Hipsters watch this movie once every six months and get chills when the theme song is played. De Niro hams up the role of a fugitive named Tuttle. Or is it Buttle?

13. *Valley Girl* d. Martha Coolidge (1983) More pompous Hipsters won't admit it, but this film rules.

14. *Delicatessen* d. Jean-Pierre Jeunet and Marc Caro (1991) A technical accomplishment of rare visual splendor that displays an unbelievably surreal apartment complex and lots of prime cuts of meat.

15. *Blow-Up* d. Michelangelo Antonioni (1966) A mod photographer during the sexual revolution in London thinks he has photographed a murder. A great film for Hipsters who enjoy debating existentialism while looking at boobs.

16. *Barton Fink* d. Joel Coen (1991) The Coen Brothers are brilliant. Polits enjoy watching the satirization of William Faulkner, who discusses writing scripts for wrestling movies when he isn't vomiting up gin in a toilet. All of the Coens' other movies are deck too.

17. *Dazed and Confused* d. Richard Linklater (1993) This film's soundtrack captures the Foghat era better than any other. Beer bongs, catty cheerleaders, and even mullets look cool in the hands of Linklater. This absurd classic helped launch the careers of Milla Jovovich, Joey Lauren Adams, Ben Affleck, Renée Zellweger, Matthew McConaughey, and Hipster favorite Parker Posey.

18. *Pink Flamingos* d. John Waters (1972) John Waters has a talent for being trashy and disgusting, and *Pink Flamingos* pushes the limits of bad taste with a white-trash cast that includes the incomparable drag queen Divine. Who knew watching people eat dog shit could be so much fun?

19. *8 1/2* d. Federico Fellini (1963) The use of midgets and circus sequences by other art-house directors is usually pretty fin, but in the hands of Fellini these devices are intoxicating. Use the term "Felliniesque" to impress your film geek friends. The prequel *Seven*, which starred Brad Pitt, is pretty cool too.

20. *Rushmore* d. Wes Anderson (1998) With the deckest soundtrack of the nineties, *Rushmore* defined Wes Anderson as the quintessential Hipster director for today's savvy filmgoer. Thank God they didn't let star Jason Schwartzman's band appear on the soundtrack.

21. *Faster, Pussycat! Kill! Kill!* d. Russ Meyer (1965) Postfeminists and those who delight in kitsch declare this soft-core gem ahead of its time. Most just like all the buxom cleavage on display. This is what happens when a film director isn't breast-fed as a child.

22. *Do the Right Thing* d. Spike Lee (1989) This is Spike Lee's only essential work. Rosie Perez's dance number to "Fight the Power" sets the pace for a film that bottled a summer heat wave better than any effort before or after. Radio Raheem should have changed his PE tape from time to time, but is a badass nonetheless.

23. *Blue Velvet* d. David Lynch (1986) Isabella Rossellini naked and Dennis Hopper with a gas mask. Deck.

24. *The Seven Samurai* d. Akira Kurosawa (1954) Forget those wimpy light-saber battles and *Crouching Tiger*. If you want to see some badass sword fighting, *The Seven Samurai* will not disappoint. One of the most influential action movies ever made, it leaves poseurs like John Woo and Jerry Bruckheimer blushing.

25. *The Apartment* d. Billy Wilder (1960) *The Apartment* star Shirley MacLaine was actually cute before she got into crystals. This is Wilder's most uproariously funny comedy. Has anyone ever used the term "uproarious" outside of a review?

26. *The River's Edge* d. Tim Hunter (1986) The one film where Keanu actually acts, but this film truly belongs to Hipster favorite Crispin Glover (no relation to Danny), who plays a charming speed freak.

27. *Gimme Shelter* d. David Maysles (1970) Regardless of your age, gender, or sexual preference, it's impossible to walk away from this amazing cinema verité documentary without having a crush on Mick Jagger. The parts where the Hell's Angels become unruly are particularly disturbing, but this is nonetheless one of the deckest documentaries ever made.

28. *Touch of Evil* d. Orson Welles (1958) Forget *Citizen Kane;* this is Welles at his best. Required viewing for fans of film noir. Who knew Charlton Heston was Mexican?

29. *Night of the Hunter* d. Charles Laughton (1955) Those LOVE and HATE tattoos on Robert Mitchum's knuckles are even cooler than Radio Raheem's rings, inspired by this classic.

30. *Naked Lunch* d. David Cronenberg (1991) Smoke up and enjoy this literary mind-fuck. Cronenberg captures the essence of Burroughs and surprises everyone by placing Robocop in the lead role.

Hip Contemporary Artists

Matthew Barney	Nam June Paik
Vanessa Beecroft	Raymond Pettibon
Jeremy Blake	Rob Pruitt
Louise Bourgeois	Pipilotti Rist
Maurizio Cattelan	Matthew Ritchie
Rineke Dijkstra	Alexis Rockman
Inka Essenhigh	Sarah Sze
Damien Hirst	Rosemarie Trockel
Barry McGee	Bill Viola
Chris Ofili	Andrea Zittel

Matters of the Heart:
Dating a Hipster

As in all matters, the Hipster strives to date fashionably. Hipsters are insular in their dating practices and usually date other Hipsters exclusively. Dating outside the genus rarely occurs.

The true Hipster is open to same-gender dating. Bisexuality is not necessarily an attribute, but openness to *bisexual potential* is something the Hipster strives for. It is very important that heterosexuals embrace this potential, regardless of whether or not they actually pursue bisexual encounters. Homophobia is midtown.

Choosing a Look

Flock of Seagulls:
Is This Style
Deck or Fin?

Answer: This style is fin.

What Hipster Men Want

Hipster males want sex. Being a Hipster doesn't outweigh being a dumb, horny boy. Women who are into bands like Gang of Four and the Fucking Champs are marriage material.

What Hipster Women Want

Hipster women no longer desire small, sensitive, sickly men in tight T-shirts. In fact, they *never* really found such men to be desirable. They just had few options during the indie-rocker era of the nineties.

Women now want small, sensitive, sickly men in tight T-shirts who know how to talk tough and embrace their masculinity. Cronkites who don't like sports are marriage material.

Popular Hipster Pickup Lines

- Your studio or mine?
- Fuck off, cunt. (Appearing aggressively misanthropic is an easy way to woo a potential hookup. The term "cunt" is genderless to the Hipster, making this come-on useful to men and women alike.)
- Didn't we meet at the WTO march?
- Did you get your tattoo done at _____? (add name of tattoo parlor)
- Wanna see my slides sometime?
- Do you like GBV?
- I like seaweed and fresh greens.
- Got any weed?
- Waddup with all the losers here?
- I bet you'd look hot in jodhpurs.
- I was hanging out in this neighborhood before it got gentrified.

Some Common (and Uncommon) Pairings in Dating

Similar to compatible and incompatible astrological signs, certain Hipster personality types are more compatible than others. Find out which personality types sizzle as we document the hits and misses of Hipster dating.

The WASH and the WASH
*Chance of Success: **Good***

As noted earlier, this match is very common and can be an exceptionally steamy one. However, the romance is often stymied when one partner discovers that his/her companion has already slept with a good portion of his/her friends. WASHes who work together have been known to part ways when one refuses the favor of subbing out a shift for the other.

The WASH and the UTF
*Chance of Success: **Poor***

This combination is generally short-lived. The WASH and the UTF have famously hot one-night stands, but the WASH quickly grows tired of the UTF upon discovering the financial status hidden behind his/her thrift shop duds. Longer flings run into a wall when the WASH has to meet the parents, who immediately ask the WASH what he/she does for a living. Plus, WASHes are inexperienced and clumsy on mopeds and have to cancel travel plans when they can't find a cheap enough fare on Priceline. There are usually too many setbacks for this match to work.

The Schmooze and the Teeter
*Chance of Success: **Hit or miss***

An unlikely match for longer affairs, but this pairing does occasionally occur. Schmoozes are at first resistant to being called "dawg" or "shorty," but enjoy the way they can let their guard down with Teeters. Schmoozes never feel competitive with Teeters and secretly

Hipster Dating Rules

- A complacent stare is better than a longing look.
- Only date people with a good record collection, so you can expand your own.
- Revealing creepy fetishes in public is for losers and Wiccans.
- If you sleep on the floor on an exposed mattress, invest in sheets.
- Don't get up to change the music in the middle of making love.
- Strive to be self-deprecating.
- Don't use pet names like "baby cake lips" in public.
- Go dutch in the early phases. Paying for someone else on a first date is suburban.
- Don't address your date by his/her last name (gym teacher style).
- Guys who refuse sex are deck.

admire their lack of ambition. When the chemistry is strong, they feel their hearts patter at the sound of approaching skateboard wheels on the pavement. Schmoozes often hide Teeters in their apartments and refuse to tell their friends that they have met someone. This relationship is always very physical and too hot to expand upon in print.

The Schmooze and the UTF
Chance of Success: Excellent
With the UTF, the Schmooze finds a soul mate. They both understand that money makes the world go round and can network with one another in the aftermath of a hot love session: "That was so hot,

baby, you always satisfy my body. Who did you say you know at Miramax?" The Schmooze's career-oriented sensibilities are subdued by the leisurely disposition of the UTF, and the two enjoy taking long trips to exotic locations to get away from it all. Problems may arise when the check comes and they can't decide whose gold card to use.

The Loner and the WASH
Chance of Success: Poor
The Loner rarely gets past first base with the WASH. Loners are generally too bashful to express their feelings for outspoken WASHes, and things fizzle out before they even develop. The WASH gets turned off when the Loner cuts a date short because they want to run home to watch *Señor Moby's House of Music.* An unlikely match.

The Bipster and the WASH
Chance of Success: Excellent
Both outspoken and intolerant of the ostentatious, WASHes and Bipsters are wonderful matches. They similarly despise corporate America and believe that people with too much money have sticks up their asses. Both enjoy going to a park on a summer day and pointing out lame people. On the downside, Bipsters always want a

quickie before leaving for work and are disappointed by the WASH's insistence upon sleeping until ten A.M.

The Bipster and the Schmooze
Chance of Success: Poor
A meaningful relationship between these two personality types is rare. Bipsters become contentious when exposed to the self-promoting agenda of the Schmooze. Schmoozes are turned off by Bipsters, who have little to offer them vocationally. Bipsters occasionally take pride in the successful conquest of a more condescending Schmooze, but they rarely fall for them. They are usually content to keep a Schmooze as a notch on their utility belt.

The Polit and the Teeter
Chance of Success: Poor
Polits and Teeters rarely meet. Polits loathe physical activity and don't ride skateboards. They also avoid dance clubs and bars where they are forced to stand, clubs of choice for the Teeter. Polits do occasionally mingle with Teeters, when they want to score a quick

A Bipster and a WASH

bag of weed, but telling their friends they are sleeping with their pot dealer never sounds good. Polits are often lured in by their sexual appeal, but ultimately opt for more cerebral conversation.

The CK-1 and the CK-1
*Chance of Success: **Poor***
CK-1s think other CK-1s are cheesy. They tend to date straight Hipsters who are experimenting with their sexuality. CK-1s have, however, been known to give each other oral sex occasionally.

The Plush Carpet and the Metal Carpet
*Chance of Success: **Excellent***
A match made in heaven. Metal Carpets love being the aggressor and enjoy seducing more coy Plush Carpets. Codependency can become a problem, though, since Carpets save most of their insecurities for behind closed doors, but the sex is always intense. Flexibility is the key to success with this pairing. The Plush Carpet should learn how to shoot pool and the Metal Carpet should wear a dress from time to time when the Plush Carpet wants to take control. With a little work, and a trip to Vermont, this match can last forever.

The Neo-Crunch and the WASH
*Chance of Success: **Poor***
Neo-Crunches are idealists who get hot talking about Walt Whitman. WASHes have a similar response discussing the work of Charles Bukowski. See the problem? Plus, Neo-Crunches are often shooed away by WASHes when trying to sell records and crafts in front of their places of business. Being escorted away with a broomstick is usually a turnoff.

The UTF and the UTF
*Chance of Success: **Excellent***
UTFs often seek out the familiar in life and can be quite happy with other UTFs. Unfortunately, the UTF's parents often disapprove if they think they're of a higher social class than their children's potential in-laws. In some cases, UTF parents have even been known to dissuade their children from continuing their affairs. Similarly, the UTF's siblings may become jealous of the matching

and prefer that their brother or sister date a Bipster, a Loner, or someone else they can look down upon. UTFs who refuse to let their passions be thwarted by their families will be rewarded with a perfect mate.

The UTF and the Clubber
Chance of Success: None
UTFs are generally a few years older than Clubbers and feel they are too old to do horse tranquilizers. Sometimes, UTFs hook up with a friend's little brother or sister who is a Clubber. Needless to say, this is rarely discussed openly.

Choosing a Look

Le Punque: Is This Style Deck or Fin?

Answer: This style is deck.

The Clubber and the Clubber
Chance of Success: *Good*

A perfect couple, though the glitter all over the sheets can be quite a mess to clean up. Both have enormous sex drives since they are young and still new at love. Plus, they are both commonly on E, which acts as a catalyst for their passion. Clubbers who date fall quickly in love with one another and enjoy hugging for hours on end.

The Teeter and the Bipster
Chance of Success: *None*

This pairing has never occurred. Bipsters think graffitti and skateboard culture is juvenile and "faggy." Teeters are afraid of Bipsters.

The Teeter and the Clubber
Chance of Success: *Hit or miss*

The Teeter and the Clubber are a common pairing. Both types are carefree and idealistic, and they enjoy making MP3 mixes for one another. They frequent the same parties, listen to the same music, and enjoy borrowing each other's clothes. Clubbers often fall hard for Teeters and are disappointed when their pages are not returned. Teeters are generally happy dating Clubbers, but stop calling after being teased by other Teeters for spending too much time away from their ramps and spray cans.

Celebrities Hipsters Have Crushes On

Men	Women
1. The Naked Chef	1. Christina Ricci
2. Beck	2. Laura Prepon
3. Edward Norton	3. Meg White
4. Ben Stiller	4. Chloë Sevigny
5. Luke and Owen Wilson	5. Reese Witherspoon
6. Any member of the Strokes	6. Gillian Anderson
7. Conan O'Brien	7. Naomi Watts
8. Jon Stewart	8. Sofia Coppola
9. Edward Burns	9. The twins from Múm
10. Mr. Big	10. Franka Potente
11. Ryan Adams	11. Audrey Tatou
12. Johnny Knoxville	12. Brittany Murphy
13. Cornelius	13. Thora Birch
14. Gael García Bernal	14. PJ Harvey
15. Jimmy Fallon	15. Selma Blair
16. Jason Lee	16. Miho Hatori
17. Joaquin Phoenix	17. Lisa Bonet
18. Steve Malkmus	18. Parker Posey
19. Jake Gyllenhaal	19. Claire Danes
20. Jeff Tweedy	20. Liv Tyler
21. Ichiro Suzuki	21. Janeane Garofalo
22. Tobey Maguire	22. Winona Ryder
23. Savion Glover	23. Asia Argento
24. Peter Krause	24. Tyra Banks
25. Bret Nicely	25. Sarah Silverman

Dating a Non-Hipster

Hipsters who date non-Hipsters are not as uncommon as one might think. In fact, this type of relationship can even be very rewarding, given the age-old adage that opposites attract. Hipsters are sometimes drawn to individuals who are borderline-deck, and occasionally date non-Hipsters with the intention of converting them. Many non-Hipsters become bewitched by the Hipster's refusal to conform to convention.

Hipster women commonly tire of Hipster men who are pretentious or unkempt, and develop crushes on more traditional men. Many Hipsters consider falling for preppy men who look like Matt Damon or Ben Affleck deviants, but it is a well-documented phenomenon nonetheless. Likewise, Hipster men often find the forbidden fruit of a sorority girl or a personal trainer to be the sweetest of all.

Hipsters will find there *are* advantages to dating non-Hipsters. Most Hipsters become more well-rounded and less condescending when forced to socialize in mixed groups that include Republicans,

A Hipster Dating a Non-Hipster

actors, bankers, and people who believe in God. They can also find pleasure in being considered the most outrageous person at the party when mingling with their lover's non-Hipster friends. Being emancipated from the homogeneity of their usual group of Hipster friends can also be a breath of fresh air. The sex is generally great too, since Hipsters enjoy sharing their sexual knowledge with the less experienced.

On the downside, dating a non-Hipster can mean being forced to listen to Sugar Ray, going to church, or vacationing on cruise ships. Hipsters are also reluctant to bring non-Hipster partners to their favorite hangouts, since their wardrobes immediately give them away as outsiders. Walking into a metal bar while wearing a baseball cap and a tie can be quite embarrassing for everyone involved.

Lines Non-Hipsters Use to Lure Hipsters

- You must be an artist.
- I only drink microbrews like Amstel Light and Sam Adams.
- Ever read any Wally Lamb? I love alternative literature.
- It's so nice to see hooters that aren't made of silicone.
- I'm into electronica, especially Moby.
- Can I buy you a Bahama mama?
- I want to get a tattoo but can't decide on the design.
- Aren't you in my yoga class at Crunch?
- I'm into kinky shit like 9½ Weeks.
- Have you accepted Jesus as your personal savior?
- Wanna go to a kegger?
- I like all kinds of music.
- Does your tongue ring make things feel different?

Hipster vs. Non-Hipster
Dating Preferences

	NON-HIPSTERS	HIPSTERS
Vacations	Going on a cruise of the Bahamas	Taking a food tour of France
	Disneyland	Renting a motorcycle and traveling across Spain
	A Sandals resort package deal	Touring the pyramids in Giza
A date movie starring	Sandra Bullock, Tom Hanks	Audrey Tatou, Luke Wilson
Set the mood with	*Chariots of Fire* theme song, Sade, Enya	Zero 7, Astrud Gilberto, Peaches, Amon Tobin
A romantic dinner location	The Olive Garden	A French bistro
Want to meet the parents	after three months	never
Favorite Sunday morning activity	going to church or mass	Reading the newspaper
	going to the gym	fucking and eating
Perfume	Shalomar, Dewberry, Liz Claiborne	none
Cologne	English Leather, Chaps, Old Spice	none

The Aging Hipster

Some say age is a state of mind—usually *before* they try on that skimpy miniskirt or extra-tight T-shirt they loved to wear when they were twenty-one. Unfortunately, aging is as inevitable for Hipsters as it is for anyone else.

The cruel reality is that once you hit thirty-five or so, many consider you a cultural relic. There is no Hipster fountain of youth, and reading *Vice* or *Paper* won't knock the signs of time from your face. Let's face it: there are limitations on how hip you can be once you hit a certain age. Even Hipster icons like Lou Reed and Laurie Anderson suffer from Hipster depreciation.

As Hipsters enter middle adulthood, they are faced with a number of challenges. Since most aspects of popular culture are intended for the twenty-something set, the aging Hipster often has trouble

Aging Hipsters: Who's Still Deck?

DECK	FIN
Tom Waits	Paul McCartney
Martin Amis	Tom Robbins
Joan Jett	Cher
Clint Eastwood	Jon Voight
Nancy Sinatra	Dionne Warwick
David Lynch	John Waters
Ang Lee	John Woo
Ted Nugent	Gene Simmons
Maury Povich	Regis Philbin
Samuel L. Jackson	Denzel Washington
Isabella Rossellini	Shirley MacLaine
Art Garfunkel	Paul Simon

staying deck. Out of sheer frustration, some move into the mainstream by joining the PTA, voting Republican, and buying mini-vans.

Many UTFs become greedy and sell out the way Jefferson Airplane did when they changed their name to Starship. They purchase stock in Motorola, subscribe to the *Wall Street Journal,* and fade into Hipster obscurity. Neo-Crunches join green markets and co-ops and spend more time planning the perfect macrobiotic meal than selecting their outfits. Polits often become professors and put *Beowulf* on their syllabus in place of Sontag and Pynchon. Loners stop buying

Hipster Dad

new records and become addicted to *Behind the Music,* often forgetting to change their cat's litter for months on end. And serotonin-depleted Clubbers go into rehab and start taking Prozac.

Other aging Hipsters continue acting and dressing as if they were still twenty years old, seemingly oblivious to the fact that they look pretty fin prancing about town in baggy jeans and shirts that say "Porn Star."

There is no definitive age marking the onset of Hipster depreciation. For many, symptoms begin in their mid-twenties. Others remain in peak form well into their late forties. Regardless, we have some helpful clues that will help you decipher whether or not you are suffering from this debilitating social illness.

Symptoms of Hipster Depreciation:

- You wear earplugs when going to a club or complain that the music is too loud. And why, you ask, does the headlining act have to come on so damn late!
- You wear long sleeves to cover your tattoos.
- You no longer know where to find drugs, and aren't even sure which drugs the kids are taking these days.
- You feel like a geriatric alcoholic when you go to a bar.
- All of your important musical influences had embarrassing comeback tours at outdoor arenas fifteen years ago.
- All of your friends are couples and have babies. You have a cool hat collection.
- You are afraid of teenagers and worry about your physical well-being when around groups of them.
- You play the Gipsy Kings when entertaining guests and listen to NPR's *New Sounds* to keep up with what is cutting edge.
- Your friends all worry about you because you don't have a 401(k). You don't even know what that is.
- You think Letterman is cooler than Conan.
- Your parents have stopped smiling lovingly when they describe you as "the eccentric one," and they say things like, "We always knew he/she would turn out differently than _____(insert sibling's name)."
- You belong to a co-op and frequent greenmarkets.
- Instead of going to clubs and parties on a Saturday night, you invite friends over to play Pictionary or go to a karaoke bar.
- You *don't* think those girls on *Sex and the City* are pathetic losers.
- You call the cops on the people next door whenever they throw a party.
- You know who Deney Terrio is.

Keys to Aging Gracefully

So, you may be asking yourself, is the term "middle-aged Hipster" an oxymoron? Our answer is a resounding NO! Aging Hipsters are

Choosing a Look

Wingers:

Is This Style

Deck or Fin?

Answer: This style is fin.

everywhere, and many of them are very deck. Forget the younger kids; those spoiled brats may not want to admit it, but you are an icon of cool and they look up to you. Here, we'll say it for you to clear the air: *You are Deck! Fuck the kids!*

Nonetheless, it is important to be aware of your age. Never try to act like you are still a part of the younger generation. Embrace your age. You are wiser. You are smarter. You are saggier too, but who cares?! You still have heat.

Since there is no manual on how to remain hip as you age, we want to provide some tips. Follow our instructions and no one will ever question your Hipster relevance.

Quit Smoking

Hipsters should quit smoking when they are thirty. Yellow teeth are never fashionable, and you want to avoid sounding like Kathleen Turner or Keith Richards. If you have to worry about your kids stealing smokes from you, you are definitely too old to be puffing. Once you do quit, don't look down upon those who still smoke. Doing so is fin. Besides, you can learn to enjoy the secondhand smoke.

Fashion, Flab, and the Perfect 'Do

A major precept of aging gracefully is to stop dressing like you are twenty-five. All Hipsters go through a transition phase when they realize that the clothes they've been wearing for the past decade no longer fit their aesthetic.

We recommend staying in shape so that you continue to look good in your wardrobe. Getting a little flabby comes with age, but you don't want to look like you have nightly spoonfuls of pig lard for an after-dinner snack.

Older Hipsters should avoid being overly flashy or kitschy. If you are over thirty-five and still wear bowling shirts, people will not realize you are being kitschy and will just assume you hand out shoes at the bowling alley for a living. We endorse solid colors and more tasteful attire.

If you want to display a little Hipster flair, *accessorize* like you are twenty-five. A pair of *CHiPs* sunglasses, some Vans sneakers, or a bald eagle belt buckle can be the perfect touch.

It's also important to get a stylish 'do. Vibrant dye jobs, streaks, and big afros are fin once you pass your peak. Nothing is more senseless than applying Rogaine to a receding mohawk. We recommend shorter cuts in slight disarray, but mops can also work for the right cronkite. For tassels, a shoulder-length cut can be stylish, but blow-dried bobs (think Monica Lewinsky) will make aging Hipsters look like they should be anchoring the local news.

Laziness Is Not Cutting-Edge

If you don't have one already, get a job. It may have been "bohemian" to live off of others when you were in your twenties, but come on.

Dressing for Work

Since most older Hipsters have careers and no longer punch a time clock when starting their day, dressing more "adult" becomes a necessity. If you need to dress more formally for work, get tailored suits. Pleated pants and khakis are for frat boys. Women's dress suits that aren't formfitting will make you look like you are an audience member of *The 700 Club*. Men should learn to tie their ties using the Windsor knot. Women should not wear pumps or fishnet hose.

Most important, wearing old, moth-eaten dress clothes to work (like many aging Hipsters do) will make you look like the man who runs the elevator in your building and pisses himself. Put your clothes on hangers instead of in a pile with a greasy plate on top. Invest in an iron.

On another note, many aging Hipsters have careers that allow them to work from home in their underwear and slippers. If you are of this persuasion, you probably own one fancy outfit saved exclusively for weddings and funerals. *Have it dry-cleaned after every social event.* Arriving in stained and smelly duds (an infamous tendency for this breed of Hipster) is never fashionable.

Rogaine Rock

If you are a member of the post-thirty-five set, our advice is this: Quit the band. Any musical aspirations you had in your youth should stay there, as fond but distant memories. Jamming occasionally can be fun, but if you give your group a name or play gigs, you've crossed the line.

Affairs and Flings

Hipsters don't buy Camaros or sleep with baby-sitters and pool boys when having a midlife crisis. Car fetishes are fatuous, and extramarital affairs are bourgeois. Not happy? We recommend acquiring a gambling habit until your partner no longer wants to be with you. If this doesn't work, find Jesus. Nothing will break up a Hipster marriage quicker than being born again.

Older Hipsters who are single should fight the impulse to score with younger Hipsters. Put out the vibe and let them come to you. Otherwise you run the risk of being pegged as creepy.

If you are already having a fling with some young hotty, we suggest keeping it casual. Never date someone who is a generation younger than you are. Getting liquid with a younger tassel or wally can be a blast, but leave it at that and move on. Dating someone substantially younger won't make you look hip; it will make you look like a pedophile.

Hipsters with Children

Many Hipsters have babies, which is frankly never deck. It's tough to look cool with baby vomit on your Joy Division T-shirt. And skipping the White Stripes show because you can't find a baby-sitter won't improve your status. But hey, if you're really fresh, you may want to pass those genes along. It would be a tough world to live in if everyone had non-Hipster parents.

Having a baby will automatically depreciate your Hipster status, but there are some things you can do to keep the damage under control. Most important, don't talk about your babies. Sure, they're cute and cuddly, but nobody cares except you. Hipsters should also refrain from boring others with baby pictures. In fact, when possible, avoid admitting you have children at all.

Finally, don't buy designer or vintage baby carriages. The terms "hip" and "baby carriage" never belong in the same sentence. Babies don't care what stroller you choose; for all they know it's a shopping cart with some cardboard on the bottom.

Aging Hipsters and the Arts

When it comes to film, music, literature, and the arts, the main thing to keep in mind is never to get lazy. Many older Hipsters feel fatigued and become too preoccupied with their careers, homes, and families to seek out hip culture. Instead of digging a little bit deeper to discover what is currently fashionable, they settle for the obvious. Here are a few things aging Hipsters should be wary of when feeling out of touch culturally.

- Never read books recommended by Regis and Kelly or Oprah. They don't know what they are talking about. What's next? Dress tips from Jerry Springer? Indie-rock suggestions by Dr. Phil?
- Don't buy greatest-hits records. If a band has a greatest-hits collection, they are already passé. Having too many greatest-hits records will only emphasize that you discovered a band too late in the game. Read reviews (you used to do it) by informed writers and choose wisely.
- Never see a film because Roger Ebert has given it a thumbs-up. His thumbs may be in the air, but his head is in his ass.
- Finally, keep going to galleries and openings. The Smithsonian is for historians and children. Since most gallery curators are Hipsters, you will be exposed to current work by artists who have heat. Plus, going to galleries will provide an opportunity to mingle with other Hipsters and inspire you to keep doing your own art.

Abide by these simple rules, and the battle against Hipster depreciation will be won.

You're Not Twenty Years Old Anymore

- Lose the backpack.
- Using grocery bags as luggage is for college students.
- Embrace the fact that baby boomer bashing is fun, even if you are a baby boomer.
- Accept that being PC went out with *thirtysomething.*
- Procrastinating on tying the knot *too* long calls attention to your age.
- If you are thirty, you are too old for a roommate.
- Stop taking money from your folks. You'll get it soon enough when they die.
- Wear a bra.
- Avoid hyphenated last names when marrying. They are a pain in the ass.
- Never dance in public, except at weddings.

But Enough Already . . .

We'll stop telling you what not to do. The most important thing to remember is to stay young at heart and have fun. Maybe it's time to put away your Sony PlayStation and stop dressing like you are a member of Sleater-Kinney, but *you are never to old to be a Hipster.*

The Questionnaire:
Are You a Hipster?

I think I'm deck . . .

Choose **one** answer for each of the following and tabulate your score at the end. No peeking at the answers! Note: Most questions have more than one correct answer.

1. **When shopping for a new pair of casual shoes, you are most likely to buy which one of the following brands?**
   - A. New Balance
   - B. Rockport
   - C. Adidas
   - D. Puma
   - E. Birkenstock

2. **You've just adopted a male French bulldog. Which of the following would you most likely name him?**
   - A. Lassie
   - B. Mr. Snuggle Teeth
   - C. Kit
   - D. Spunky
   - E. Jimmy

3. **When at a cocktail party, other Hipsters are trying to out-clever one another exchanging remarks about their favorite eighties tough guys. You interject with your personal favorite:**
   - A. Judd Nelson in *The Breakfast Club*
   - B. Dolph Lundgren in *He-Man*
   - C. Dennis Hopper in *Blue Velvet*
   - D. Richard Dean Anderson in *MacGyver*
   - E. Sylvester Stallone in *Rambo II*

4. **When planning a Saturday night, which of the following would be your first choice?**

    A.   Dinner at Chi-Chi's followed by a movie at the local multiplex

    B.   Attending an art opening

    C.   Muddin' in your jacked-up truck, down by the power lines

    (D.) Going to a speakeasy club where absinthe is served

    E.   Staying at home to watch *Walker, Texas Ranger*

5. **To set the mood on a romantic date you would play which of the following?**

    A.   The theme to *Chariots of Fire*

    (B.) A Barry White and Sade mix tape

    C.   Astrud Gilberto

    D.   The Melvins

    E.   *Songs of the Humpback Whale*

6. **You would most likely subscribe to which magazine?**

    A.   *Harper's*

    B.   *Maxim*

    C.   *Redbook*

    D.   *Wallpaper*

    (E.) *Italian Maxim*

7. **You prefer your armpits to smell:**

    A.   Powdery or flowery

    B.   Naturally musky

    (C.) Unscented

    D.   Sporty

    E.   Like pork

8. **Your dream car is**

    A.   An SUV

    (B.) A seventies Mustang

    C.   A PT Cruiser

    D.   A vintage Volkswagen bug

    E.   A Hummer

9. You go to a bar offering the following beers. Which one do you select?

    A.   Coors Light

    B.   Tequiza

    (C.) Guinness

    D.   Anchor Steam

    E.   Molsen Ice

10.   Your dream vacation with that special someone would be:

    A.   Seville, Spain

    B.   The Poconos

    C.   A Sandals resort

    (D.) Paris, France

    E.   Disneyland

11.   Which of the following most closely describes your temperament in social situations?

    (A.) Complacent

    B.   Ready to kick some ass

    C.   Perky

    D.   Paranoid

    E.   Self-deprecating

12.   The following best describes your opinions with regard to pornography:

    A.   A devout fan

    B.   It's fine for others, but not for me

    C.   It pays the bills

    D.   It causes crime and rape

    (E.) Watching seventies porn can be funny

13. **When attending a dinner party, the conversation turns to the politics of George W. Bush. You would most likely say or do which of the following?**

A. "I like Bush, but John Ashcroft is my true hero."

B. "Fascist."

C. You get a little misty and put your hand on your heart.

D. "I want to move to Canada until he is out of office."

E. "Four more years!"

14. **When spending time with a same-gender friend from high school, he/she begins making boisterous jokes about homosexuals in a public place. You respond by doing which of the following?**

A. You say, "You have a purty mouth" and move in a little closer.

B. You make some jokes of your own and give your friend a high five.

C. You begin to weep.

D. You decide to wait another ten years to see this friend again, and hope that he/she will be out of the closet by then.

E. You tell him/her that all people are equal in the eyes of the Lord.

15. **You would most likely buy a recording from which of the following artists?**

A. Insane Clown Posse

B. Korn

C. Wilco

D. Kool Keith

E. The Strokes

16. **Packing for the beach, you would most likely bring:**

A. Sunscreen

B. Suntan oil

C. A Jimmy Buffett CD

D. A thong bikini or Speedos

E. Cutoff shorts

17. **Your favorite clothing store is:**

    A.   Walgreen's

    B.   Salvation Army

    C.   Diesel

    D.   Hecht's

    E.   The Gap

18. **The computer you would prefer to use at home is which of the following?**

    A.   Macintosh

    B.   Dell

    C.   Gateway

    D.   I hate computers

    E.   Compaq

19. **Your favorite late-night talk-show host is:**

    A.   Jay Leno

    B.   Jon Stewart

    C.   Craig Kilborn

    D.   David Letterman

    E.   Conan O'Brien

20. **When visiting your local pharmacy, which of the following dental products would you most likely select?**

    A.   Tom's of Maine

    B.   Crest Original

    C.   Aquafresh

    D.   Super-grip Polident

    E.   Crest gel

21. **You prefer a home or apartment that has:**

    A.   Hardwood floors

    B.   Vinyl siding

    C.   Wood paneling

    D.   Wall-to-wall carpeting

    E.   Shag carpets

22. **Pick an appetizer from the sample menu below:**

A. Poppers

B. Wings

C. The Hungry Boy Fried Sampler

D. Bruschetta

E. Steamed clams

23. **Which of the following items are you most likely to find in your wallet?**

A. A Blockbuster Video rental card

B. A photograph of your pet

C. Bamboo rolling papers

D. A sheepskin condom

E. A ticket stub from an art museum

24. **You love date movies that star:**

A. Parker Posey

B. Tom Hanks

C. Franka Potente

D. Julia Roberts

E. Freddie Prinze, Jr.

25. **When choosing a font for your business card you select:**

A. Courier

B. You don't have a business card

C. Times New Roman

D. Helvetica

E. Martin Gothic Ultra Light

26. **You have at one time or another kissed someone of the same gender.**

A. True

B. False

27. **You have purchased a U2 record in the last five years.**

A. True

B. False

28. **The last two movies you saw had explosions in them.**

    A. True

    (B.) False

29. **You sign onto the Internet using AOL.**

    (A.) True

    B. False

30. **You have margarine in your refrigerator.**

    A. True

    (B.) False

Answers

1. A, C, D: +1 point; B, E: –1 point
2. C, E: +1 point; A, B, D: –1 point
3. C, D: +1 point; A, B, E: –1 point
4. B, D: +1 point; A, C, E: –1 point
5. C, D: +1 point; A, B, E: –1 point
6. A, D, E: +1 point; B, C: –1 point
7. B, C: +1 point; A, D, E: –1 point
8. B, D: +1 point; A, C, E: –1 point
9. C, D: +1 point; A, B, E: –1 point
10. A, D: +1 point; B, C, E: –1 point
11. A, D, E: +1 point; C, B: –1 point
12. B, E: +1 point; A, C, D: –1 point
13. B, D: +1 point; A, C, E: –1 point
14. A, D: +1 point; B, C, E: –1 point
15. C, D: +1 point; A, B, E: –1 point
16. A, E: +1 point; B, C, D: –1 point
17. B, C: +1 point; A, D, E: –1 point
18. A, D: +1 point; B, C, E: –1 point
19. B, E: +1 point; A, C, D: –1 point
20. A, B: +1 point; C, D, E: –1 point
21. A, E: +1 point; B, C, D: –1 point
22. D, E: +1 point; A, B, C: –1 point
23. C, E: +1 point; A, B, D: –1 point
24. A, C: +1 point; B, D, E: –1 point
25. B, E: +1 point; A, C, D: –1 point
26. A: +1 point; B: –1 point
27. B: +1 point; A: –1 point
28. B: +1 point; A: –1 point
29. B: +1 point; A: –1 point
30. B: +1 point; A: –1 point

What Your Score Means: How Hip Are You?

    –30 points–0 = **Irredeemably fin**

    1–10 points = **Milquetoast**

    11–20 points = **Poseur**

    21–25 points = **On the Precipice**

    26–30 points = **Deck**

Fuck your lame test = **Punk Rock**

Behind the Scenes:
It Takes a Village

About the Author

Robert Lanham is the author of the romantic series known as *The Emerald Beach Trilogy*, which includes the works *Precoitus, Coitus,* and *Aftermath.* This collection of novels was recently called "a beach towel classic" by *Red-*

Robert Lanham

book. Robert has a great body and often drives shirtless in his Camaro. He brushes his teeth several times daily, but is nevertheless prone to cavities. He is currently the editor of *FREEwilliamsburg,* which can be found on-line at www.freewilliamsburg.com. He lives in Brooklyn, New York, and works at Foot Locker on the weekends.

About the Art Director

Bret Nicely's theories linking artistic practices with sandwich making buttressed much of the cultural output of the early twenty-first century. His work *Poststructuralist Beer 'n' Brat* won the 2002 Turner Prize and was named a "Best One-dish Meal" by *Gourmet* magazine. Bret began work-

Bret Nicely

ing with Robert Lanham through their shared interest in falafel, and in 1999 became the chief creative officer at *FREEwilliamsburg*. He lectures widely around the world and currently lives in Brooklyn.

About the Drawer

Jeff Bechtel

Jeff "J-dawg" Bechtel grew up on the cruel streets of Richmond, Indiana. As a teenager, he battled an addiction to glue and took up drawing to escape the thug life. He was recently called "the greatest drawer of his generation" by Phil Donahue. His work has appeared in *Dutch*, *Maxim International*, and "Family Circus." He currently lives and works in Brooklyn.

About the Content Assistant

Mandy Novak is originally from Freeport, Maine, but relocated to Brooklyn, New York, in 1997. She is too deck to comment on further.

Mandy Novak

Additional Credits:

Creative Consultants—Anna Brown, Jaimie Canavan, Glenn Coan-Stevens, the perpetually hip Kristen Fulton Wright, Sarah Gilbert, Dan Kilian, Kevin Kraynick, Jud Laghi, Alexander Laurence, Julia Lazarus, Vu Ong, Ned Rote, Rasha Refaie, John Rickman

Photographer—Turge Stout "B.S." Nicely
Models—Alex Shimo-Barry, Karen Russo, Josh Burton
Fashion Director—Jill Spector
Manicurist—Amy Brown
Fiber Optic Splicing Technician—Ariana Souzis
Staff Yenta—Elyse Kaplan
Computational Physicist—Cameron OBrion
Cardio and Thoracic Surgeon—Matt McLean, Ph.D.
Barmaid—Ann Toebbe
Bioinformatics Researcher—Noah Sussman
Manager of Advanced Rock Systems—George Koelle
Master Accessorizer—Kristen Jenson
Molecular Diagnostician—Joanna Burgess
Director of Ornamental Plant Research—Colin Cheney
Fluffers—Sally Michaelson, Chris Parker, Doug Simmons
Key Grip—Shaun Wright

An abbreviated version of *The Hipster Handbook* originally appeared in *FREEwilliamsburg*.

FIN

Choosing a Look

The Björn Borg:
Is This Style Deck
or Fin?

Answer: This style is deck.